WHICH
WAY
TO
GOD?

Ronald E. Sleeth

WHICH
WAY
TO
GOD?

Nashville   ABINGDON PRESS   New York

WHICH WAY TO GOD?

Copyright © 1968 by Abingdon Press

Library of Congress Catalog Card Number: 68-11474

Scripture quotations unless otherwise noted are from the
Revised Standard Version of the Bible, copyrighted 1946
and 1952 by the Division of Christian Education, National Council of Churches, and are used by permission.

SET UP, PRINTED, AND BOUND BY THE
PARTHENON   PRESS,   AT   NASHVILLE,
TENNESSEE, UNITED STATES OF AMERICA

Dedicated to

HAROLD HERMANN

who first suggested this book
and who individualizes for
me the many faithful laymen
who have crossed my path

"There is not just one way to God, as there is to an oasis across the desert or to a new mathematical idea across the breadth of the science of number. For man there are as many ways of approach to God as there are wanderings on the earth or paths to his own heart."

Jacques Maritain

PREFACE

A young man once refused to join the church because he was afraid to become a Christian. He was in a pastor's membership class, but felt he could not become a member because he could not point to any one time in his life when he had had a Christian experience. How many of us have had the same doubt in regard to our Christian commitment? There are many people in the church today who do not understand Christian experience.

Some feel they are in the church under false pretenses because they have never been able to cite a time when a decided change came over their lives. Others have had a conversion experience years ago, but nothing has happened to their faith since. Still others joined the church under the urging of parents, and feel no joy in their Christian experience. Yet others are bored with the church, getting more out of their service clubs than from their religious fellowship. And others, feeling dispirited in their own religion, say, ''Look

7

at Mrs. Jones. What a radiant Christian. There must be something wrong with my experience, for I certainly don't feel the way she must."

In our most honest moments, most of us have had feelings similar to these, or at least have wondered where we stood in our Christian experience. All of us have seen the necessity to grow in the experience we have had.

The Christian life assumes that there has been a Christian experience, a conversion, or a new birth. We need to see, however, that there are various approaches to God, thereby understanding our own Christian experience and seeing that it is a continual growth. This book—designed especially for laymen—is an attempt to examine some of these various approaches to God. Each type of approach is based on biblical materials, with an examination of its strengths and weaknesses. It should not be assumed that Christian experience is always fragmented into specific types. They overlap. Nevertheless, it is helpful sometimes to understand the richness of faith by seeing its variety.

Yet it should be obvious that none of these approaches is mutually exclusive. A dynamic experience of maturity will embody many or several of these elements. For example, emotion may precede or accompany an intellectual decision. An intellectual faith will seldom be devoid of feeling. Nurtured faith may have still other facets.

The main thing is that God works in many ways. He takes us where we are. He calls us to grow in our own experience. He challenges us to enlarge our own vision by examining the various ways of faith. While a Navy chaplain in World War II, I saw demonstrated for me this variety of religious approaches in the Christian faith on a typical Sunday. Often we would begin the sabbath with a ritualistic Communion service for the Anglo-Catholic brethren; then one or two typical Sunday morning services of a general Protestant type in a formal setting; at noon perhaps a service in the brig; in the afternoon open field services off the back of a jeep; and, finally, in the evening an evangelistic service in the little Quonset chapel. In none of these did I believe that God was dead or absent. Indeed, it was only as I stood at the end of the day and looked back over all of them did I feel that I had seen Christian experience in its richest and fullest sense. In all of these I could see God at work in various ways.

The life of John Wesley dramatizes much of what I want to say in this book. Wesley was a young Anglican priest, one of the most brilliant

9

men of the eighteenth century—a teacher at Oxford University. Although he was committed to the church, we know that his intellectual faith did not satisfy him. Later on, at Aldersgate, he felt his heart strangely warmed. This emotional conversion put fire under his intellectual commitment and sent him out to turn England upside down for the sake of Christ. But even this does not tell the whole story. For back of Wesley was the little parsonage at Epworth and the role of his mother, Susanna. Although raising a host of children, she always found time to spend an hour a week with each child concerning religious matters. That influence hovered over and affected Wesley all his life. Only after the merging of these various aspects of faith could we say for Wesley what Paul said of his religious experience, "It is no longer I who live, but Christ who lives in me."

A word of thanks to my colleague, Mr. Decherd Turner, for reading the entire manuscript with a critical and sympathetic eye. Mrs. John Norris also went beyond the call of duty in handling this material in an appreciative manner by bringing to completion what was once an illegible manuscript.

RONALD E. SLEETH
Dallas, Texas

CONTENTS

1

PIONEER CHRISTIANS

In one of the panels of the altarpiece now at Colmar, France, Matthias Grünewald has painted a striking picture of the Crucifixion. Jesus is hanging on the cross, and nearby is the figure of John the Baptist pointing to Jesus as if to say, "He must increase, I must decrease."

There is something hauntingly beautiful about the person whose life is subordinated to another's in order to achieve a greater good. The forerunner Christian—the one who does not see his own dream or role fulfilled, but who gladly points to another—is a person who captures the imagination of us all.

I

John the Baptist is the prototype for this kind of religious experience. His life is fascinating, and his importance in the Christian tradition is unquestioned. In the Gospel of Matthew we read that John came preaching in the wilderness of Judea. His gospel was one of repentance in preparation for the coming kingdom. He was likened to the prophecy foretold in Isaiah:

> The voice of one crying in the
>   wilderness:
> Prepare the way of the Lord,
> make his paths straight.

His manner was strange; he came in crude clothing and ate simple food. But his preaching was effective. People repented and came to him for baptism. He pointed his message away from himself and declared that one came after him whose shoes he was not fit to tie. Even Jesus came to be baptized by John, and although the latter was embarrassed, Jesus insisted.

We need not relate the whole story of John's ministry.[1] For our purposes we can highlight the salient features. He was an uncouth character;

14

we might say, a primitive in the tradition of Elijah. His gospel was one of judgment and repentance. He pulled no punches. Beginning a sermon with "You brood of vipers" would not be calculated to win friends or establish a long pastorate. He was fearless and confident—likening himself to the prophecy in Isaiah of one who would come to "prepare the way of the Lord." He felt the coming of the Lord and his kingdom was imminent, which no doubt added to the urgency and fearlessness of his message. Yet there was a humility about the man which was as striking as the boldness of his message. He disclaimed any divine authority for himself. He pointed to another, saying that one would come who was mightier than he.

Jesus became the one John pointed to, and Jesus paid John the highest homage by asking for baptism at his hand. It is believed that John and Jesus were related through their mothers— Elizabeth and Mary—but of much more importance was their relationship as brothers in the faith. It was at his baptism at the hands of John that Jesus was cognizant of his unique relationship to God. Thus, John's importance as the forerunner for Jesus is indisputable, even though in manner and even message they were unlike.

15

John was a fire-eater. In Mark it is stated, "Now after John was arrested, Jesus came into Galilee, preaching" (Mark 1:14). The Gospel seems to take it for granted—almost calmly—that John would be arrested. When we examine his message and manner, we see why. At one point he advised his hearers to share their clothing and their food (Luke 3:10-14). He admonished the internal revenue collectors to be fair. He told the soldiers to watch their violence and accusations. He even told them to be content with their wages. This is clearly not preaching designed to please. And, to top it off, he attacked the king for illicit marital relations. For this he was imprisoned and lost his head. John the Baptist would never be taken for Caspar Milquetoast, nor for many of his descendants in the ministry.

John's gospel should not be dismissed as an irresponsible gospel; indeed, it was a vigorous one. At one time the scribes and Pharisees tried to drive a wedge between John and Jesus by stating that the disciples of John fasted and prayed while Jesus and his disciples ate and drank—with the wrong people (Luke 5:33-35). In other words, John's disciples were seen as rigorously ascetic and disciplined. They had a pristine and primitive faith which was single-minded in its devotion.

16

The most arresting thing of all about John, however, was the subordinate role he placed himself in in relation to Jesus. Once a group of priests and Levites came to ask him who he was. He confessed he was neither Christ, nor Elijah, nor the prophet (John 1:19-23). What a temptation! To be doing well; to have a group of disciples; to have crowds responding to the preaching; and then—take yourself out of the spotlight, off center stage. He was in another place mistaken for Christ, but quickly pointed away from himself (Luke 3:15). To be able to say, literally or figuratively, at the height of one's powers, "I am not the Christ," takes inner discipline and selflessness. Yet John bore witness to another, pointing to Jesus and saying, "Behold, the Lamb of God, who takes away the sin of the world!" (John 1:29). Later on he says of Jesus, "He must increase, but I must decrease" (John 3:30).

II

If John's experience of religion were the only kind, we would have a most one-sided faith—a partial gospel. This type of experience would be primitive, representing an uncouth and unlettered approach to God. While we should never equate

17

the Christian faith with sophistication or intellectualism, neither should we expect the Christian to equate piety with primitivism or with a fanaticism born of a faith without understanding. There should be no premium given for ignorance. Particularly in certain types of evangelical Christianity has there been a trend of equating faith and emotional crudities.

Another problem with the John-the-Baptist kind of faith is that it does not represent the total gospel. It tends to be judgment and repentance without love and grace. This is one of the distinctive differences between the "religion" of Jesus and that of John. Jesus, without minimizing judgment, added the note of love—something unemphasized in the message of John. Need the lesson be drawn for our day? There are still those who make their faith a sour, judgmatic, exclusive one which seems to be nourished in vinegar. They seem to delight in the exclusiveness of their Christian experience and rejoice in the damnation of others.

This leads to the next problem with many descendants of John. Some in their enthusiasm for a rigorous kind of faith tend to want an exclusive pattern for the church. This leads to a development in church history of the "sect" movements. The sect represents a party within the church

18

which usually is of a dissenting nature from the established or parent church. The sect is often the group which pulls out and forms a new church when things don't go just right. Or it often leaves the church and follows a disgruntled minister who wants to begin a new group. The basic philosophy here seems to be that a small group which thinks alike and whose view of religion and Christian experience is the same makes that view normative for everyone. And, if the others cannot follow this pattern, then the group often forms a "splinter" church.

Further, there has always been in Christian history a tension between the prophet and the priest. The Old Testament reveals these two strains and their relationships. Although the Christian church has endeavored to keep the two together, there has always been the temptation to line up behind one or the other. This has been peculiarly a problem for the clergy as they have sought to define their own roles. John, as an itinerant preacher, has always represented the prophetic strain, while in the modern day his successor has been the wandering evangelist or the social reformer. The priest, on the other hand, has represented the settled pastor—the shepherd of the flock—who on a long-term basis attempts to meet men's needs

19

through patient ministering. These pictures are approximations, but they indicate why the church has always affirmed both roles at the same time.

A John-the-Baptist needs to be a pastor as well as a prophet.

III

A "forerunner's" gospel is important. It is the beginning. John's gospel was a necessary prelude to Jesus' gospel. There must be judgment and repentance before there can be grace and salvation. This is still true for an adequate Christian experience. Both are needed. "You can't have one without the other," and that is as true for Christian faith as it is for "Love and Marriage." Take the family, for example. Parents who bestow love without judgment are indulging in sentimentality and softness. Parents who engage in judgment without love are flirting with brutality. The Christian gospel is a gospel of love, to be sure, but it is a complete gospel—it includes the element of judgment.

Further, John's experience of religion reminds us that we need the prophetic strain in our faith. He spoke directly to the people without fear or favor. He spoke to all classes of men without any change of emphasis. Whether he was speaking to Herod, tax collectors, soldiers, or any other person, the message was courageous and forthright. Royalty or commoner, soldier or civilian, slave or free—all were addressed by the audacious words of John. Some scholars feel that Jesus' decision that he must suffer and die may have been a response to John's death. That is, when Jesus recognized where John's teachings and his courage led him, Jesus began to see the inevitability of his own end if he pursued with vigor his own ministry. The rigorousness of John's faith was important to Jesus, and is to us. Such courage is a commodity needed in every age by the Christian. His experience should include the dimension of faith which permits him to speak forthrightly on the issues of the day. He should be encouraged by John's example to speak out on the subjects of racial brotherhood, war and peace, poverty, and all the other great issues of our time. An experience which lacks the prophetic dimension will often be sentimental and soft. John's legacy to our faith, among other things, will always be the strain of the prophetic— the faith that hears the Word of God and then speaks it fearlessly.

Perhaps the most important legacy left by John is the importance and courage of pointing to an-

21

other, of being able to say "There is one who comes after who is mightier than I am." That takes great courage—and a great spirit. For a man who is great in his own right to sacrifice himself—as it were—so that someone later can triumph takes the greatest of spiritual gifts.

This motif of being a forerunner, or a sacrificial agent, is easily demonstrable in history. John Hus, Savonarola, and Wyclif were all prereformers and died for their views. In a sense, they came too early; yet they prepared the way for Luther. They did not live to see their dreams fulfilled; still, the dreams were fulfilled, and without these precursors the Reformation would not have happened or else it would have been delayed another age in history. No wonder Wyclif has been called the "morning star" of the Reformation; he and others laid the foundations upon which Luther and his followers built.

A Columbus who sails uncharted seas never lives to see the fulfillment of his discovery. The father who willingly gives up a kidney so his young daughter has a chance to live, even though it may shorten his own life span; the people in the church who vote to build a new sanctuary even though many of the older ones know they will never live to see it completed or be able to worship in it; the

22

Mickey Mantle who lays down a sacrifice bunt even though the crowds are screaming for him to "hit away"; the pioneer who takes his family across the country in a covered wagon, knowing that he himself probably won't make it to California—all these demonstrate in varying degrees the nature of the John-the-Baptist Christian. Such experiences—laying the groundwork but never seeing the completed task and sacrificing one's own life so that another may succeed—are at the heart of the Christian gospel.

It is indeed difficult to say "I am not the Christ"; to bear witness to another; to say "He must increase, but I must decrease." Yet a mature Christian faith must say that, precisely because Jesus Christ went before and sacrificed for us. In turn, we have the privilege—through God's grace —of being sacrificial and pioneer Christians for those who come after us, strengthened by our witness.

2

PRODIGAL CHRISTIANS

Prodigal is not usually considered to be a positive word. We immediately use it negatively, associating the term with the prodigal son in the Bible who wasted his inheritance by living riotously. According to the dictionary, prodigal means recklessly extravagant; characterized by wasteful expenditure; lavish; profuse. None of these—at least on the surface—looks promising as a type of Christian experience. And yet, is it not possible to consider prodigal in a positive sense? Can there be such a thing as a prodigal Christian?

I

A good example of a religious experience which has the elements of prodigality is found in Matthew 26:6-13. (See also Mark 14:3-9.) It is the story of Jesus visiting in the home of Simon the leper at Bethany. A woman—presumably unknown—came up to him and poured an expensive ointment on his head as he was eating. The disciples were outraged at this apparent waste, knowing that the ointment could have been sold for a large amount of money which could go to the poor. The disciples must have been surprised at Jesus' answer. He seemed to relegate the poor to a position not characteristic of his sympathies. He focused instead on the woman's act and commended her for the beautiful thing she did.

When we read this passage, we may characteristically mix up the cast of characters. Our sympathies are with the disciples. "What a waste! Look at the poor who could have been helped. A year's wages down the drain." This is the way we think, as did the disciples. We fail to see the story in perspective. This story is no justification for the continuation of poverty. Jesus had too many other things to say about the needy and downtrodden to allow us to believe anything like that. Here the point is that in a moment of crisis—his impending doom—this woman had chosen the better part. She did "the one thing needful." Even her motives may have been wrong. Some scholars[1] believe she

25

was one of those who hoped Jesus would set up a government with himself as the head, and overthrow the Roman regime. Jesus probably saw this accurately as a last rite of anointment for his burial. Perhaps here was another indication of his consciousness of divinity. This act could have made him aware again of his relationship to the expected Jewish Messiah. The woman saw the incident as an act of kingship, but he saw it as a preparation for burial. She may have pictured Jesus in a crown, but it was to be a crown of thorns.

At any rate, she was "prodigal" in her lavish affection for Jesus. It shocked his companions. Her great devotion and generosity were beautiful traits, and Jesus said they would be remembered after she had gone. Her burst of affection was commended rather than condemned by Jesus. As Halford Luccock points out, "She was lifted clear out of arithmetic into love—one of the greatest leaps which a life can ever take." [2]

In Luke's Gospel (7:36-50) we get a similar yet vastly different story from that of Matthew and Mark. Luke puts a parable and a story together: a story concerning a woman of the streets who anoints Jesus and washes his feet and a parable of a creditor who forgave his debtors. In a

26

real sense, Luke is using his material for an entirely different purpose from the one we have indicated. One scholar, speaking of the material in Luke, writes, ''The point of the story is that one who loves much is forgiven much; the point of the parable is that one who is forgiven much, loves much.'' [3] On the other hand, there is still the motif of love and devotion toward Jesus—extravagantly given. John Knox has an excellent insight into Luke's passage which confirms the prodigal nature of the woman's love:

The extravagance of this woman's actions—the washing of Jesus' feet with her tears, the drying of them with her hair, the kissing of his feet, the anointing of them from the alabaster flask of ointment—all of this seems appropriately to suggest the really inexpressible gratitude and love, transcending any human loyalty, which the earliest believers felt for Christ. . . . The acts of the woman were remembered and treasured because they were in a vicarious way their own acts. She did in the story just what they would have desired to do.[4]

Whether or not this is true of us, it is true that this thread of love given extravagantly is part of the Gospel record. (See also John 12:1-8.)

Similar to these stories is the one of the widow's mite, a story found in Mark 12:41-44 (also in Luke

27

21:1-4). Jesus watched rich people putting money into the treasury out of their abundance, and a poor widow came in to put in a small amount. To Jesus the widow was to be commended because she put in everything she had—not just out of her abundance. She too had a prodigal concept of faith. "There was something in her heart that lifted the gift out of routine into the realm of sacrifice." [5] Precisely, this is the nature of the prodigal experience of faith. John Henry Jowett tells of a graveyard near a little church where some devoted soul evidently gave untiringly of her life and spent her life recklessly. Her epitaph read: *"She hath done what she couldn't."* [6] What a wonderful slogan for a prodigal Christian!

II

The type of Christian experience suggested here is one which frightens most of us—at least it would if it were considered normative. Most of us have a disliking for the fanatic in religion as well as in anything else. Our vision of the prodigal-type Christian may well be some newspaper report of a man who "got religion," left his family to fend for themselves, quit his job, and went off to be an evangelist. There are enough examples in history

28

of this kind of behavior to make most of us wary of religious experiences which are excessive. For example, in the last century an Adventist group led by William Miller expected Christ's imminent return to earth. Consequently, it is reported they sold or gave away their properties, dressed in white robes, and waited expectantly on the day of Christ's supposed return.

The story of the great Leo Tolstoy has similar overtones. He was a wealthy landowner and outstanding novelist. Yet at an advanced age he espoused a simple piety which was based on love. He tried to live a perfect life in regard to charity for others. In so doing, he gave up his estate, renounced the copyrights on his books, and never had a penny to call his own for the rest of his life. Such behavior appalls most of us, even if done in the name of religion. We do not want our religion to be so extravagant that it becomes embarrassing. Most of us, anyway, do not feel that our religious experience calls us to such extremes.

To state it bluntly, we are glad that there have been extraordinary Christians such as Kagawa or Albert Schweitzer; yet most of us do not feel called to go to Lambaréné or to the slums of Tokyo. We feel that at best we are going to be Christian, if at all, in the circumstances in which we find ourselves.

29

We of course do not feel that extraordinary Christians are "fanatics." Most of us just recognize that our Christian commitment is seen in light of our other loyalties; for example, family, friends, and vocations. In *The Cocktail Party* by T. S. Eliot, a psychiatrist in advising a sensitive young woman who seems to feel a sense of meaninglessness sums up life—and the Christian life—for most of us: "I can reconcile you to the human condition," where many of us live who

> Maintain themselves by the common routine,
> Learn to avoid excessive expectation.[7]

This is the level on which we live religiously, avoiding fanaticism and even extreme devotion. Figuratively and literally, we just do not feel called to Lambaréné.

III

Nevertheless, the church has always had the extraordinary Christian who has been prodigal in his devotion. Whether we call them "saints" or not, we are all grateful for those who have "wasted" their lives in the name of Jesus Christ. Whether it has been Father Damien in the leper colony of

Molokai, Kagawa in the Japanese slums, or Schweitzer in an African hospital, we are all inspired by the Christian life which goes all the way in its extravagance for the sake of the gospel. The young woman referred to earlier in Eliot's play decides she does not want to be reconciled ''to the human condition,'' but wants to take the way of suffering and sacrifice. For her it ended in death, as she was killed by the natives in a far-away land. Such prodigal faith is always an inspiration to us, and the lives of extravagant Christians have throughout history fertilized the soil in which the seeds of our faith have flourished.

But beyond the fact that prodigal Christians inspire us as we look at their lives, there is something about extravagant Christianity that calls all of us to do something about the pedestrian nature of our own religious experiences. For most of us, fearing fanaticism in faith, settle for a lukewarmness. We tend to give no more than necessary of ourselves, our money, or our time. We become legalistic in doing what is necessary, but nothing more. Halford Luccock describes most of us accurately when he writes, ''Personality is a precious perfume. . . . Life slips by and the perfume jar is never broken. Others always measure themselves out with a medicine dropper, frightened lest

31

they spend a drop more than the legalities of the situation demand."[8] But prodigal Christianity cannot exist on a delicately balanced scale; it throws itself away in devotion. William Wordsworth, in "Inside of King's College Chapel, Cambridge," caught the spirit of spilled-out faith:

Give all thou canst; high Heaven rejects the lore of nicely-calculated less or more.

For the nature of prodigal love rests ultimately on the nature of God's love toward us. We see this kind of love most dramatically in the parable of the prodigal son in Luke 15. There is a sense in which the parable is misnamed. The story could just as well be called "The Prodigal Father," for it is really about him. He is the point—the climax of the whole parable for Jesus. For the father here represents God, and it is his love which is prodigal according to Jesus—spilled out, given without limit, unreservedly. There are many ways in which we see this love in this particular story, but one of the most graphic is the way in which the father accepted the younger, repentant son. It is seen in one of the most beautiful lines in all literature: "While he was yet a distance." The father *ran* to meet his son, ready to accept him; full of mercy and compassion, he enfolded the son in his arms. Here is another side of "The Hound of Heaven" to whom Francis Thompson likened God. This time not pursuing with . . .

> Those strong feet that followed, followed after.
>> But with unhurrying chase,
>> And unperturbed pace,
> Deliberate speed, majestic instancy,
>> They beat.

Here God is not chasing, but reaching out, receptive, forgiving, spilling out love prodigally. How difficult it is for us to understand this kind of extravagant love.

Suppose, though, we knew of a family where there had been unfaithfulness on the part of the husband. The family circle was broken, the children were crushed, and the wife was brokenhearted. Now there is nothing that the husband can do to restore the family relationship. He cannot buy his way back into the family. The only way the family can be restored is if the wife out of her agony decides to for*give* him—the heart of for*give*ness being *gift*. But suppose the wife does forgive him and the family relationships are restored, and strangely there is a deeper understanding than was there before—not a forgive-

33

ness that never forgets and brings up the past, but a love that reaches a depth that erases the act of unfaithfulness and grows strong in a deeper love. How difficult it is for us to imagine this on a human level such as marriage! How much more difficult is it to see God's relationship to us in its forgiving love. Yet it is precisely this kind of love that the Christian talks about when he talks of God.

The cross is a difficult symbol for most of us, but it is precisely this prodigal, spilled-out, suffering love that we see in or on the cross. And when we look at it, we find it hard to explain what all it means; but our hearts fill with love, a lump comes to our throats, and we sing in response to this suffering love:

> Were the whole realm of nature mine,
> That were an offering far too small,
> Love so amazing, so divine,
> Demands my soul, my life, my all.

3

PROXY CHRISTIANS

One of the great Reformation doctrines is the familiar *saved by faith alone.* Sometimes, to be more exact, we say that we are saved by grace through faith, not works. A close corollary to that doctrine ought to be—for anyone's reformation—*saved by the faith of others.* For, if there is anything that is clear, it is that we either have our first Christian experience or are nurtured in the one we have by the faith of other Christians. Conversely, our own faith sometimes consciously or unconsciously will lead others into a Christian experience.

I

The New Testament is full of incidents where the belief of someone else seems to be more im-

35

portant than the experience of the one who comes to faith. A classic example of faith by proxy is found in Mark 2:1-12. (Cf. Matt. 9:1-8; Luke 5: 17 ff.) It is the story of Jesus at Capernaum, preaching in a crowded household. A paralytic was brought by four men who had to let the stretcher down through the roof because of the crowd. Jesus, of course, healed the man. There are many interesting facets to this story. For one thing, Jesus upset the scribes in his audience by forgiving the man's sins before he healed him. They were not interested in the healing of the lame man. They were more concerned with the blasphemy of saying "My son, your sins are forgiven." Thus, the nature of Jesus' authority is one dominant theme here. The other one for our purposes is within the narrative itself. It concerns the four friends who carried the crippled paralytic, removed the roof, and let their friend down into Jesus' presence. The Gospel states, "And when Jesus saw *their* faith, he said to the paralytic, 'My son, *your* sins are forgiven' " (italics mine). The striking thing about this healing story is that nothing is said about the faith of the man who was healed. He could have been a religious man, it is true, but he could have easily been an agnostic, an atheist, a man of no faith. That did not seem

36

to enter the picture in any way. What was important was the *faith of his friends*. They went to a great effort to get their friend to Jesus. If they did not climb mountains, they at least tore off roofs. They had unquestioning faith in Jesus' ability to heal their friend. And he did.

Later on in Mark (5:21-24, 35-43) there is the story of Jesus raising Jairus' daughter. Jairus, a ruler of the synagogue, came to Jesus and fell at his feet beseeching him to come and heal his daughter. "Come and lay your hands on her, so that she may be made well, and live." Here again, there is no faith on the part of the child but tremendous faith on the part of the father, who did not seem to doubt in the least Jesus' ability to save his daughter. The scene changes quickly. As they approach Jairus' house, they learn that the little girl is now dead. Jesus calms the parents' fear and says to the father, "Do not fear, only believe." Here again, no faith is demanded of the child, but faith is asked only of the father. On this basis Jesus restores the little girl to health.

The same pattern is found again in Jesus' relationship to the mother of a child (Mark 7:24-30). Jesus was trying to stay in a house incognito, but a woman who had a sick child heard of his presence, came to the house, and fell at his feet. She

37

was a Greek, a foreigner, but evidently had faith that Jesus could restore her child's health. The enigmatic parable in the midst of our story concerning the bread thrown to the dogs and dogs eating crumbs need not trouble us here. It is believed Jesus was trying to tell the woman of his primary ministry to the Hebrews, but her answer suggests her faith was ready to be given for any small favors to a foreigner. When she returned home, the demon had gone from the child. We do not know whether the child had faith or not; the mother had plenty.

Jesus' healing of the blind man in Bethsaida (Mark 8:22-26) portrays the same motif. The Gospel states, "And some people brought to him a blind man, and begged him to touch him." Jesus did by spending some time with the man, placing spittle upon his eyes, and asking him if he could see. When the man's vision remained dim, Jesus proceeded to lay his hands upon him again until the sight was fully restored. In all this time, even though there is conversation reported, not a word is said about the man's faith. But it is obvious that those who brought him to Jesus had the faith.

Once more Jesus encounters a father whose son has epileptic seizures (Mark 9:14-27). The disciples had tried to help but could not, and now the father was bringing the boy to Jesus. Jesus reminds the father that all things are possible to him who believes. The father cries "I believe; help my unbelief!" The focus here is on the father's faith, not the son's. Belief is necessary but obviously not for the one being healed. The boy may not have had any; the father did, no matter how plagued with doubts he might have been.

One other scene in the Gospel of Matthew further demonstrates the faith of others (Matt. 8:5-13). A centurion approaches Jesus and asks that he help with a sick servant. As Jesus starts to go with him, the soldier states that he is too unworthy to have Jesus in his house. Yet what a faith! He states that Jesus can save the servant by just saying the word. Jesus is amazed and says that he has not found such faith in all Israel. He was so impressed by the man's faith that he said to him, "Go; be it done for you as *you have believed*" (italics mine). The servant was healed—not through his faith but through that of his master.

II

The gospel record, then, is quite clear in affirming that we are saved by the faith of others. But this is not the only way to approach God. Indeed, by itself it would be a most inadequate way. In other places in the Gospels, Jesus is just as much concerned with the faith of the one seeking salvation as he is in the foregoing instances of the friends, parents, or masters of the ones receiving help.

There is certainly a danger of living off another's faith without having one of your own. Many people in churches today are there because of the faith of their parents which led them there or keeps them there. But not all these people have a satisfactory experience of their own. This is why so many of these people are unhappy churchmen. They have accepted the beliefs of the parents—out of respect, perhaps—without appropriating faith for themselves. Faith of others may lead to God and help us stay there, but we need to assume that faith for ourselves if the Christian religion is to have real meaning in our lives. Over the long run, we cannot accept the fruits of faith without the roots of faith.

We must have an experience of our own to live a mature Christian life. We cannot have an enduring faith by proxy. A father, a mother, a husband, a wife, children, a boss, an employee—all these might lead us to God, but ultimately we need a faith of our own. In the wedding ceremony the

40

minister reminds the couple that "no other vows [are] more sacred than those you now assume." The same can be said for church membership or Christian experience. The deepest experience belongs to us alone—no one else. Just as dying is our own personal experience, so is the deep, satisfying experience with God. It is ours alone.

III

Yet, as the Gospels have shown, the faith of others in our own experience cannot be overemphasized. Good friends or even casual acquaintances can have a lasting effect on our Christian lives. As a youngster, I remember a Sunday school teacher who crossed my life briefly and left an indelible mark. His name is forgotten, as well as many physical details. Yet his discussions of alcohol stayed with me through the years and conditioned my own thinking when I had to deal with that problem in my college days. He spoke against drinking not on biblical or even moral grounds but on the premise that in a competitive society a man must keep his mind alert to function effectively. Since he was a successful businessman, I was impressed as a youngster with his reasoning. Although I might see the problem now in an entirely

41

different manner, I cannot forget the influence on my own life of another person.

Or, take parents. Seemingly wayward children will often break their hearts through the "wild years" of youth, bringing pain and anguish to distraught parents. Yet they are often shocked but pleased to discover that later in manhood or womanhood—under some crisis—the son or daughter begins to perform with responsible action learned in earlier years at the parents' side. So the prayers of mothers for wayward sons which are oft-repeated are not farfetched as some of the stories would lead us to believe. The influence of one life on another cannot be overestimated, even though it may not be readily apparent.

In Acts 5:12-16 there is a fascinating story about the influence the early church leaders had on the people. In this instance it is Peter, and we read these interesting words:

And more than ever believers were added to the Lord, multitudes of both men and women, so that they even carried out the sick into the streets, and laid them on beds and pallets, that as Peter came by *at least his shadow might fall on some of them.* (Italics mine.)

Just think—they hoped his shadow would fall on them. The influence of a shadow! What a question to ask of all Christians. What would the influence of my shadow be like? Would my shadow falling on someone influence him in any significant way? Think for a moment of the influence of athletes on young people. What a tremendous responsibility and privilege to have one's shadow thrown on a youngster—an influence that might affect his life for good or ill forever. The thought of our responsibilities as Christians is frightening and awesome. Yet as Christians, this is our burden and opportunity.

Home on leave during World War II, I was waiting in one of the offices of a large company. I picked up the house magazine. In the page devoted to letters I discovered a letter written by a sailor to his old boss at the firm, telling of a chapel service in the Pacific which had changed his life. My eyes bulged as I read, for it became plain that it had been a service which I had conducted. I left that office with a feeling of sinful pride, perhaps, but mostly an awesome awareness of the significance of one Christian's influence.

The theme of the faith of others in Christian experience is one of the basic elements at work in intercessory prayer—not only the belief in God who can answer prayer but also the belief that we can influence him on behalf of others. President

Willis Tate of Southern Methodist University tells the incident of a group of friends who believed that prayer and concern can change things. This small, informal group of men decided they could do for another much more than he could do for himself. "We chose (without his knowledge) one man for whom the group held great esteem and one that we believed to be capable beyond his current assignment, and we decided that we would keep this man on our prayer list and go out of our way to say encouraging words to him and about him and the results were amazing."

Yes, our lives may be transformed by the influence of others; and, in turn, it is our witness as Christians to let the shadow of our influence fall on the lives of others.

4

EMOTIONAL CHRISTIANS

If most of us were absolutely honest with ourselves, we would have to admit that our Christian experience is largely emotional. We consider our faith to be in the realm of feeling, the same as love or patriotism. There are good reasons for such a claim. The history of the Christian church is emblazoned with the names of those who have experienced God in an emotional way. Indeed, since religion deals with the will, it is only natural to suppose that our experiences of God are all, in one way or another, on the level of feeling and emotion.

I

One of the most dramatic, emotional experiences of religion in history is the story of the conversion of Paul in Acts 9. Paul, originally named Saul, had been an ardent persecutor of the Christians. He had stood by at the stoning of Stephen. He had been raised a strict Pharisee and was an intellectual pursuer of truth. Yet here on the road to Damascus, within the twinkling of an eye, he became a changed man. The details of the story are familiar to all Christians. As he journeyed on the road, a light from heaven flashed about him, and he fell to the ground and heard the voice of Jesus speaking to him. This experience with Jesus was real to Paul and transformed his life. The men with him heard the voice but did not see anyone. Paul was struck blind for three days and neither ate nor drank. It would be difficult to find in all of history a more cataclysmic example of a religious conversion. This experience was so real to Paul that he felt he had been in the presence of the Master as had the disciples.

While Paul's conversion is perhaps the most dramatic experience in the New Testament, there are indeed others which are in a similar vein. Although the details are skimpy, it seems safe to say that even the calling of the disciples must have had the quality of a sudden, emotional experience for those who came in contact with Jesus and straightway followed him. Jesus said to Simon and Andrew, "Follow me and I will make you become fishers of men" (Mark 1:17). And *immediately* they left the nets and followed him. The same with the sons of Zebedee who *straightway* followed Jesus.

Not only in Scripture but also in church history have the pages of history recorded conversions which seem to be emotional in their suddenness and intensity. Augustine's conversion is well known and is recorded in his *Confessions*. He was a profligate young man who was skeptical of things religious. Yet one day in a garden he heard the voice of a child from a neighboring house say "Take up and read." Feeling himself addressed by these words, he turned to Romans 13:13-14. From this moment Augustine had peace of mind and felt the indwelling presence of divine power. His life was changed completely by this surge of feeling which altered his life.[1]

Some such experience as Paul's or Augustine's has been duplicated in lives of Christians throughout the ages. To a greater or lesser degree, many Christians have found their experience to be of a similar nature. Representing an emotional approach to faith, it corresponds to the decisions made at altar rails during adolescence by a host of Christians in America, especially in the South. It is the type of religion associated with revival meetings of a bygone day and with Billy Graham today. It is often associated with a pietistic, conservative theological background, but it need not be so. The same religious phenomenon is found in youth camps at campfire services or vocational commitment retreats irrespective of geography or theology. Whether a youth retreat in Michigan or an old-time revival service in Alabama, the phenomenon is the same. A person, by whatever motivation—be it preaching, music, emotional appeals, testimony—feels his own guilt and unworthiness in the face of the claims of the gospel, repents, and feels the release which accompanies forgiveness.

Many Christians would admit that their religious experience is of this emotional quality. That is not to say that there are no other elements within their faith, but it is to affirm that the primary principle is the one of feeling or emotion. Indeed, it would be difficult for anyone to affirm that his religious experience is devoid of feeling. To do so would be similar to saying that a marriage is without love.

48

II

In our day particularly, there has been a great reaction against emotion in religion. With a few exceptions, the churches have reacted to the excesses of revivalism, especially in regard to emotion. The reason for this has its roots in the nineteenth century. In the days of the revivals on the frontier with their undoubted good, many historians spoke critically of the "acrobatic Christians"—those who jumped, yelled, cried, and ran around "jerking" as they "got religion." In our day we have revolted against such unseemly behavior in our religion and have discarded both the revivalism and the emotion. In fact, it is probably true that through the years some have disregarded religion itself because of these emotional excesses. In any event, many modern churchmen are skeptical of emotion or emotionalism in their faith, and they are skeptical because of the emotions associated with camp meetings and revivals.

Close to this is the divisiveness of revivalism which disgusts many Christians. One man, telling of the experiences of his youth, said, "Each year we had a revival in our church. An evangelist was brought in, and he trampled on the emotions of the adolescents and tried to scare the old ones with the

49

fear of Hell. But the worst part was the attitude of those who were 'saved.' They seemed to believe that if you didn't 'feel' as they did and 'experience Christ' as they had, then you weren't Christian. Their own 'feelings' seemed to be the standard for establishing whether a person was Christian or not. It took our saintly pastor about a year to get the church back in shape."

Yes, there has undoubtedly been a divisiveness connected with revivalism's emotionalism, especially at the point of suggesting that a certain kind of experience or feeling is necessary or normative for all Christians. I know one man, reared in such a geographical area, who has never become a Christian primarily because he is still waiting for some "thunderbolt" emotional experience which will make him a Christian. In the meantime, he is not in the fellowship of the church.

In short, there is a danger of confusing *emotion* with *religion*. Roy L. Smith once told of being approached by a woman in North Carolina who told him that she didn't like her new minister. "Why not?" asked Dr. Smith. "Well, I've been to hear him three times, and I haven't cried yet." Dr. Smith commented that what this woman needed was an onion, not a sermon. She was confusing religion with a certain kind of feeling. We cannot confuse heartburn with a heartwarming experience. And particularly in our day, we should be skeptical of any religion which claims to be sufficient without intellectual grounding. An emotional faith devoid of tough-mindedness will not suffice for the twentieth century. It cannot command the minds and hearts of the modern-day man.

III

On the other hand, it is equally clear that the modern man—no matter what his affirmations—cannot get along without emotion. In order to get rid of the excesses of emotion, we may have thrown the baby out with the bath water. We need to see the values of emotion in our faith. Indeed, we need to see the indispensability of the emotional experience of religion. One of the first ways to do this is to see that there is a difference between *emotion* and *emotionalism.* The former connotes the level of feeling which is indispensable in human, as well as religious, relationships. The latter implies excess. One minister reported that after being reared in an area which was known for emotionalism in religion, he went through a period in his ministry in which he would not quote a poem in a sermon for fear that it would be too emotional and

51

therefore would deal with his congregation's feelings unfairly. He said that he had to come to see that there was a difference between emotion and emotionalism. The former is warm and basic; the latter is cheap and tawdry.

Another way we can see the value of the emotional approach to God is through the test of the experience itself. If an experience which is largely emotion-centered results in a dedicated life of sincerity and new life in Christ, then no one can quarrel with that experience. "By their fruits ye shall know them," and nowhere is this more true than in one's daily Christian life. If that changed life came about through the depths of one's being and through the feelings, then we must applaud the resultant life without condemning the experience which brought it all about.

A group of young seminary students were sitting around discussing their future ministries. Most of them, hoping to be parish ministers, expressed a desire to be relevant and concrete preachers. By this, they were saying that they wanted their congregations to hear the gospel unadorned and apart from emotional appeals or tawdry use of their people's feelings. In other words, they were expressing their distrust of substituting emotion for faith in religion. One of the

52

men, listening to the discussion but saying little, finally spoke. "I agree with you fellows. I too hope the faith I preach will appeal to men's minds, but I keep remembering my father's conversion. He had led a drunken and wasteful life. Yet he was converted in a Billy Sunday revival, and from that time on his life was completely and forever changed." Yes, even while recognizing the excesses of emotion in the realm of religion, we affirm that feeling as the dominant force in certain people's faith has changed their lives.

One young minister in the same group told about his relatives in the Appalachian Mountain area. His point was that, granted that the faith of many of these people was emotional, it worked and produced faithful Christian lives. He said that they might be "short on book larnin'" but that they were "long" on living faithfully in their day-by-day relationships with one another. Again, their faith rooted in feeling produced Christian lives.

The crux of the kind of experience being described here can best be illustrated in a comment of Dr. Roland Bainton which was made in another connection. I once heard him say, in speaking of preaching, that in the modern pulpit there was an "absence of a strain of tears." He did not mean, of course, that preachers should be more

53

tearful or that they should try to get people to cry. (Remember the woman who needed an onion?) Dr. Bainton is suggesting that the modern-day pulpit is in danger of losing its capacity for feeling deeply. He is reminding the preacher that while faith is not feeling alone, it has a great deal to do with feeling. What Dr. Bainton said about preaching could be said about religious experience itself. The "strain of tears" refers to the deep wellsprings of emotion which motivate us in our Christian experiences.

The most important thing to recognize is simply that religious faith can never be divorced from the realm of feeling, for it is in our emotions that our wills are touched and we are motivated into action. Besides, what would our faith devoid of feeling look like? Can you imagine a family which tried to operate without emotion? Picture a parent dealing with children by making an intellectually derived list of each child's faults, then punishing the one with the longest list. No, the family operates in the context of love, enfolding all the children, punishing, to be sure, but wrapping up together faults and virtues in the overriding concern of love. This is what real religion is. A man's religious life is never settled by what his theology is or how well he *knows* his catechism. His final test is this: "As you did it to one of the least of these my brethren, you did it to me'' (Matt. 25:40). The motivation for such action comes from faith springing out of feeling. Without this emotional undergirding, it would be like packing the car for a vacation but having no gas in the tank.

Toscanini, the great symphony conductor, once said of musicians, ''Trouble with most musicians, they have such big heads and such little hearts. They know so much but feel so little.'' This would be a sad epitaph for anyone's religious experience. A great experience of faith, of course, has both elements. An exciting Christian experience is one which is *convincing* and *moving*.

5

SHALLOW CHRISTIANS

Suppose we were to hear that another Dead Sea Scroll had been found—a fifth Gospel, the *Gospel According to Judas*. Even before the old parchment was unrolled, it would be interesting to speculate how it would look. Have you ever thought how Judas' Gospel would read?

Judas' villainy has always tended to obscure the fact that he was, after all, a disciple of Jesus. Remembering only his betrayal, we sometimes forget that he was personally selected by our Master to be one of his disciples.

I

The climax of Judas' career is on the night of the Last Supper in Jerusalem. Jesus is eating with his disciples and predicts that one of them will betray him. They all disclaim any such intention but nevertheless ask "Is it I, Lord?" Judas, along with the others, asks the same question. Later, Judas kisses his Master in the presence of a mob, and they seize Jesus. Still later, Judas sees his condemnation, repents, and even tries to give back his paltry thirty pieces of silver. The chief priests and elders refuse to accept "blood money" in the Temple, so Judas throws the money on the floor, storms out of the Temple, and hangs himself.[1]

The obvious question is, What happened to Judas? Why did one of the disciples choose to betray his Master? Did Jesus himself make a mistake in selecting his close followers? What really happened we, of course, do not know. Yet much of the story can be reconstructed[2] by inference. Jesus undoubtedly chose Judas—as he did the others—because he saw possibilities of nobility and great usefulness. Judas at the beginning probably responded with great enthusiasm to Jesus and his ministry. It is thought that Judas was well accepted, perhaps even the treasurer of the group. Some think he may have been sitting directly beside Jesus at the Last Supper.

But why then did he betray Jesus? Scholars

have suggested many reasons for this act. One of the most reasonable suggests that Judas became disillusioned with Jesus for not acting with messianic zeal in upholding the laws and institutions of Judaism. Judas wanted him to be the Jewish Messiah, preserving and purifying the law but not changing or abrogating the law. In other words, Jesus did not live up to Judas' expectations.

We too often ignore Judas because his crime was so heinous. Yet we need to remember that he was a disciple and, disturbingly enough, we have some relationship to him. He was a disciple of Jesus, one who betrayed him to be sure, but he also repented. Even after his betrayal and death, Judas was evidently considered to be "one of them." The disciples chose a successor for Judas, saying, "for he was numbered among us, and was alloted his share in this ministry" (Acts 1:17).

If Judas had left a Gospel, he would not have been the only character in it. He would have plenty of company in his Gospel. Many "disreputable" characters have been close to Jesus one way or another. Think of Matthew—a hated tax collector who became a disciple. Jesus seemed to have an affinity for the unlovely. He ate with the sinners and tax collectors. One of Jesus' greatest sins.

58

according to his contemporaries, was the company he kept.

Pilate might be in the *Gospel According to Judas* but not because of his relationship to Judas in the events of Holy Week. Pilate is a symbol for many Christian disciples then and now who are disinterested—men who try to remain on the sidelines and not get involved. He was a "wash-the-hands-of-the-whole-thing" disciple who knew Jesus wasn't guilty but who wanted to stay out of the proceedings. He didn't want to get involved. He hoped the whole issue would somehow disappear.

Even Peter could get at least one chapter in Judas' Gospel. We remember how he told Jesus that he would never desert him and was shocked when Jesus said he would deny him three times that very night. Well, Peter slept when he was supposed to be awake watching, he denied Jesus three times, and he repented and wept. Sounds similar to his brother disciple Judas, who kissed his Lord, betrayed him, and wept.

Yes, Judas would have company in his own Gospel. Ananias and Sapphira could get a few verses. They kept back part of the price which was due the Christian community (Acts 5:1-10).

59

How many others could get in this particular Gospel?

II

It is difficult at first to see Judas as an example of an approach to God—except on negative terms. His was a cosmic tragedy, forever etched in the annals of history as the crime of crimes. What greater crime could there be than to betray his Master? Perhaps only one other crime could compare—he also betrayed himself.

Jesus indicated the kind of Christian whom Judas represents. In the parable of the sower Jesus speaks of the types of soil in which the seed is planted:

Other seeds fell on rocky ground, where they had not much soil, and immediately they sprang up, since they had no depth of soil, but when the sun rose they were scorched; and since they had no root they withered away. (Matt. 13:5-6.)

The temptation to relate this passage to Judas is almost too great to resist. Yet Jesus gives his own interpretation of his figure:

As for what was sown on rocky ground, this is he who hears the word and immediately receives it with joy;

60

yet he has no root in himself, but endures for a while, and when tribulation or persecution arises on account of the word, immediately he falls away. (Matt. 13:20-21.)

Judas was indeed a "rootless" Christian whose earlier enthusiasm was abandoned because he had no root in himself. Rootless or shallow Christians have always been with us; Judas has his friends. Tom Paine saw the same kind of people during the Revolutionary War. For him, they were the "sunshine patriots": "These are the times that try men's souls. The summer soldier and the sunshine patriot will, in this crisis, shrink from the service of his country." [3] Substitute *Christ* for *country* and you have Judas and his tribe.

Yet in spite of all the things that can be said about Judas, it is clear that his act in the drama of the gospel not only made the Crucifixion necessary but the Resurrection possible. It would be too much to affirm that he had to betray Jesus as part of a divine plan, but given the betrayal, it became part of the divine drama which unfolded—all of one piece. Kazantzakis even suggests the necessity of Judas' role when in his story of the Passion he has a priest who is trying to enlist a villager to play the part of Judas speak, "Without Judas, no Crucifixion, and without Crucifixion, no Resurrec-

61

tion. It's therefore absolutely necessary that one of us should sacrifice himself and take the part of Judas."[4] Whether necessary or not, it is true that most of us "take the part" of Judas in some way or another in our lives.

III

Judas' villainy makes obvious the negative aspects of his discipleship, but can we gain anything positive from him to aid our approach to God?

First of all, we should remember that Judas was a disciple of Jesus. The Master chose him and loved him. Before we too hastily condemn the Judases around us and in us, we should be reminded of the closeness between our Lord and Judas.

Also, we need to recognize that, just as Judas' sin was great, so was his repentance. It was twisted in its fanaticism (like his betrayal) and led him to take his own life. But it is not too much to suppose that even he was forgiven. The One who could forgive the thief on the cross could certainly forgive his betrayer and former friend, especially since there was repentance.

These lessons alone should be helpful to us in our experience, but there is more. We need to remember that Judas' Gospel is our Gospel at times. This is where we are in relation to our Lord. We may not feel that Judas' role is as important as Kazantzakis felt it was when he has a character say:

For the world to be saved, Christ has to be crucified. For Christ to be crucified, someone has to betray Him. For the world to be saved, as you see, Judas is indispensable, more indispensable than any other Apostle. . . . He's the one that's most necessary, after Christ.[5]

Whether Judas was indispensable or not, we do not know. We do know that Christian disciples continue to betray their Lord. Whenever we let prejudice rule our lives, we betray him. Whenever we let a political party, national policy, or anything else take priority over the Master, then we have betrayed him and have let Judas' Gospel become our Gospel.

So Judas' question "Is it I, Master?" is a universal one. It is still being asked—or should be. "Is it I, Master, who betrays you a hundred times a day through indifference, pride, or self-idolatry?" Even the kiss—a symbol of closeness—is significant in this regard. Judas used that gesture to betray his Lord. Oscar Wilde caught his infamy

63

in these lines from "The Ballad of Reading Gaol":

> Yet each man kills the thing he loves,
>   By each let this be heard,
> Some do it with a bitter look,
>   Some with a flattering word,
> The coward does it with a kiss,
>   The brave man with a sword!

Maybe those of us who call ourselves disciples—those closest to him—are the very ones who do betray him the most often.

To go back to the *Gospel According to Judas* with which we started, suppose one was found. What would it read like? Unfortunately, it would probably sound like a Gospel according to you and me. But fortunately, the same grace that redeems even a Judas is there for those of us who are his brothers. That grace, where repentance is present, loves us, forgives us, and restores our relationship to him.

6

INTELLECTUAL CHRISTIANS

Phillips Brooks gives a fascinating account of his first days in a divinity school. He had come from a college where men studied hard but said nothing about faith. His first experience with a prayer meeting came at the seminary, and he was impressed with the devoutness of the young men. However, the next day in the Greek class he noted that some of the most devout men were unprepared in their lessons. Brooks comments that "the boiler had no connection with the engine." [1] Reflecting on this incident after many years in the ministry, this great preacher observes, "In many respects an ignorant clergy, however pious it may be, is worse than none at all." [2] If we take the

priesthood of all believers seriously, then what
Brooks points out about the clergy could well
be true for all Christians. The Christian church
has never put a premium on empty-headedness.
Indeed, it has always tried to keep in a close relationship devotion and intellect—the boiler and
the engine.

I

One of the clearest examples of the intellectual
approach to God is the biblical account of the conversion of the Ethiopian eunuch in Acts 8:23-40.
This fascinating story tells of Philip, an ardent
disciple, and his meeting with a prospective man
of faith. The eunuch, a foreigner, was seated in his
chariot reading, of all things, from the book of
Isaiah. Philip asked the important traveler if he
understood what he was reading. The man replied
that he could not understand unless he had guid-
ance. Philip sat down with him and, beginning with
the Isaiah passage, he told him the good news of
Jesus Christ. The eunuch accepted this explana-
tion, believed the gospel, and asked for baptism.

Not many pastors could match Philip's success
and speed in gaining a convert—from an initial
contact to baptism in one visit. But apart from the

details of the narrative, it is interesting to compare this incident with Paul's conversion which comes immediately following in Acts 9 and which we have already considered. Here there is no blinding light, no falling to the ground, no voice, no blindness. The gospel evidently makes sense to the eunuch, and he decides to become a Christian.

Theodore P. Ferris, discussing Philip's encounter with the eunuch, says:

What Philip found was this: He found a man who was seeking something, diligently, sincerely, earnestly, not self-satisfied, reaching out for something more than he had ever known before, and yet a man not understanding what it all meant. This was Philip's great opportunity.[3]

And so it has been throughout Christian history: men "not understanding what it all meant," and the gospel presented so as to meet their needs and increase their understanding. The mark of this approach is the endeavor to show Christianity's reasonableness.

Even Paul, whose conversion was used to illustrate the emotional approach to religion, could be cited in this category of "intelligent Christian." To see Paul thus is perhaps paradoxical, but not contradictory. For he was a "man for all seasons," a character with many facets, not the least of which was a powerful mind. He argued his own case in courts, he disputed with the religious leaders who opposed him, and in connection with our present category we see him most vividly in his visit to Athens (Acts 17:16-34). Paul adapted to his audiences, and with the Epicureans and Stoics of Greece his approach was on the rational and intellectual plane. G. H. C. Macgregor says of Paul's adaptability:

There can be no doubt that Paul went to great lengths to find points of contact with his hearers' ways of thinking. To the Jews of Pisidian Antioch he traced God's purpose in their history; to ignorant pagans at Lystra he spoke of God revealed in nature; and now to the cultured Athenians he strives to demonstrate philosophically that the new Christian religion of revelation is the perfect fulfillment of the religion of reason common to all mankind.[4]

Paul complimented the Athenians on their religious quests and then sought to reason with them that the one God who made heaven and earth could not be worshiped in stones. Therefore, Paul attempted to make known as the Father of all men the unknown God he had seen the Greeks worship.

Even though the ending of his speech doesn't seem too successful (he didn't leave a church in Athens, some mocked, and only a few listened seriously), we cannot be too sure of Paul's impact. His approach, while evidently not immediately rewarding, may have planted seeds which bore fruit in the Greco-Roman world just because Paul's reasoning appealed to the minds of some in that intellectually advanced area.

Such a rational, intellectual approach to God is not unusual in the Christian church. Many Christians base their faith on a set of intellectual principles. To them Christianity makes sense. It is a sound philosophy of life; the best way to live. Horace Bushnell saw the importance of the intellectual decision many years ago. He relates that

A young man, correctly but not religiously brought up, light and gay in his manners, and thoughtless hitherto in regard to anything of a serious nature, happens accidentally one Sunday, while his friends are gone to ride, to take down a book on the evidences of Christianity. His eye, floating over one of the pages, becomes fixed, and he is surprised to find his feelings flowing out strangely into its holy truths. He is conscious of no struggle of hostility, but a new joy dawns in his being. Henceforth, to the end of a long and useful life, he is a Christian man.[5]

69

Such an experience can be duplicated by Christians in all periods of history.

Persons have discovered that in the marketplace of ideas Christianity has been tried and not found wanting. Missionaries, especially, have won converts on this level. A tribal chieftain may see the moral and social growth of people after the gospel has touched their lives. He may then along with his whole tribe become converted to this new way of life. The testimony of these Christians is that you do not have to subjugate the mind to be a follower of Christ. Theodore P. Ferris states it aptly when he affirms: "The mind of man is as important in religion as it is in mathematics, for religion not only moves a man to feel deeply but it also moves him to make up his mind about the universe and his own place in it." [6]

II

The limitations of a solely rational religion are as obvious as any one-sided approach to faith could be. In the last chapter we saw the danger of too much heart and too little head. See the obverse here. A brain without a heart can be a cold and forbidding organ. The Christian who places all his eggs in an intellectual basket makes a serious blunder in understanding man's nature—his own included. Unconsciously, at least, he is taking man not where he is but where he would like for him to be. The assumption—expressed or not—is that men's minds are suspended in vacuums and that bombarding them with ideas *about* God will give them an experience *of* God. We do not have to be trained psychologists to know that man is not mind alone, feelings alone, or anything else— *alone*. He is a bundle of things—mind, emotions, feelings, hates, prejudices, and so forth. The so-called rational man is the figment of someone's imagination. Although it would be dangerous to infer from this criticism that man is primarily irrational, it is nevertheless true that he cannot be seen primarily or solely as a reasoning being. That point needs emphasis—and in the right place. Man cannot be seen *solely* as anything. Here, then, is the problem with an intellectual's religion. He tries to compartmentalize his religion into a rational world devoid of feeling, where no man dwells ultimately.

As was said in the previous chapter, our culture is afraid of emotion, especially in regard to religion. Yet we are motivated constantly in other realms through emotional persuasion without the least qualm. We are moved by advertisers on the

71

nonrational level all the time. We brush our teeth with "Clean" which contains "octochlorophyllene." For all we know, it might be a preservative for shoe leather, but that kind of nonrational slogan sends us into the supermarket to buy "Clean." We go to a concert and expect to be raised to great emotional heights when we hear Beethoven's *Ninth Symphony.* We watch our favorite TV comedian and laugh until the tears roll down our cheeks. We go to a play and expect a Judith Anderson or a John Gielgud to move us through the gamut of our emotions. Yet we are tempted to keep emotion out of our modern churches, for we feel it is unseemly and cheap. Apart from the fact that a human being cannot be so fragmented, it should be clear that neither can religion. An intellectual faith—devoid of feeling—is a sterile faith.

III

Yet we cannot overlook the values of an intellectual grounding of our faith. Our age, as never before, needs to see the relevance of the Christian message. For example, young men and women on college campuses need to be challenged by the claims of Christ. They need to see that Christianity can stand with other philosophies of life, argue with them, and better them. They need to see that here is something which makes sense; a philosophy which they can live by, build homes on, and pass on to their children. An empty-headed religion cannot do that.

And, of course, all of us need to realize that our experience must be grounded in reasonableness in order to interpret our faith. How can we tell others about faith unless we can understand it ourselves? We often hear complaints that our children are growing up ignorant in the faith. One reason might be that they do not hear it talked about meaningfully in the home.

Someone has suggested that a belief is not a belief until it can be verbalized. This is perhaps too strong. But it does suggest that a nodding acquaintance with faith is not nearly so strong as the ability to state clearly what we believe and then live by it. An intellectual approach helps us because we cannot talk meaningfully about something which is not understood and structured rationally within ourselves. Many people have decried the passing of the old-fashioned prayer meeting. Perhaps its passing was inevitable. One of its blessings, however, was the opportunity given for people to stand on their feet and talk

73

about their faith. Such an opportunity can develop meaningful Christian experience—an indispensable ingredient in our world today.

The urgency of this task cannot be overemphasized. In a day when scientific and other areas of knowledge have jumped forward with amazing rapidity, the church cannot lag behind in the race for men's minds. The time is too crucial to smother the intellect, no matter how sincere or pious the intent. Nor can we close the mind in order to open the spirit. Someone has said the mind is like a parachute: it is no good unless open. Dr. Ferris puts it in a less quaint but no less real way: "Whenever the church closes it mind, it might as well close its doors, for at that moment it ceases to take the mind of man seriously, and man minus mind is animal." [7] The times are much too serious for turning churches into zoos.

John Wesley, spiritual father not only of the Methodists but of all who have evangelical roots, never for a moment allowed a separation of the feelings from the mind. His brother Charles spoke for both of them—and indeed for all Christians—when he wrote the now familiar words, "Unite the pair so long disjoined, knowledge and vital piety." This inscription is prominently displayed in an academic building on the Southern Methodist University campus. That is an appropriate place. So would be an altar. Such an affirmation should be one of the primary tenets of any Christian's practicing catechism. This is what Phillips Brooks was saying in his graphic image of the boiler being connected to the engine. The mature Christian can say only an Amen to that.

7

NURTURED CHRISTIANS

Horace Bushnell, a famous Congregational minister of the last century, gives us a text for the nurture type of Christian experience. Speaking out of a religious climate which assumed that becoming a Christian involved an emotional, cataclysmic conversion, Bushnell contended that such an experience, while valid, was not the only way to become a man of faith, nor, indeed, could it be considered the most normal kind of Christian experience.

His contention was that the growth of the child into the church would be a natural part of his development, without his necessarily going through the psychological wrenchings of a conversion experience. It was his belief "that the child is to grow up a Christian, and never know himself as being otherwise." [1] He believed that the child should grow up in an atmosphere so Christian that his becoming a Christian would be as natural as breathing. Bushnell's ideas—in the historical period in which he lived—placed him at variance with the prevailing opinions of religious experience. Not only that, but he shifted the emphasis away from a solely individualistic concern for faith to a more socially oriented conception of Christian faith—specifically, the responsibilities of the family in regard to the child's development and his faith. Such an idea had implications not only for the family but for the church as well.

I

The most apparent biblical corollary to Bushnell's concept of Christian nurture is in the person of Timothy—the friend and companion of Paul. In the first chapter of II Timothy are found the following words, addressed to the young disciple: "I am reminded of your sincere faith, a faith that dwelt first in your grandmother Lois and your mother Eunice and now, I am sure, dwells in you" (vs. 5). Such a passage indicates that here is a

77

faith transmitted through three generations. There is no record here of blinding lights or voices from heaven; indeed, there is no revelation of any kind of conversion experience. He seems to have grown into the faith through the witnessing and nurture of Christian relatives.

There are, of course, problems in reconstructing both the authorship of this epistle and the specific details of Timothy's lineage. Nevertheless, it seems clear that Timothy was a product of a family of faith. Says Fred D. Gealy, "Taken at face value, the text certainly supposes that both Lois and Eunice were Christians." [2] Such an affirmation demonstrates the nature of Christian families even in the early days of the Christian church. Dr. Gealy writes:

What the precise situation in the historic Timothy's family may have been, the text . . . is best interpreted as showing the writer's great confidence and joy in third generation Christian ministers, and the security he feels in the case of those who in the home have been rooted and grounded in the received (Pauline) form of Christianity.[3]

If Timothy is the best prototype we can find in the Bible for the Christian nurture type of experience, the idea of that experience is found throughout the Bible. In Ephesians 6:1-14, there is a passage which someone has suggested represents the first sign of Christian education in the home. In this particular scripture, advice is given the children in regard to reverence for the parents; and parents, especially, in regard to their children, are asked to "bring them up in the discipline and instruction of the Lord."

The motif for this kind of training is not unique in Christian literature. The Hebrew tradition, of which we are all a part, is replete with the idea of nurture. There is no need to recount at length what is obvious—the importance of the Jewish family in the Old Testament. To give but one example out of this heritage, when the Hebrews are given their commandments, the first one, of course, is the Shema: "Hear, O Israel: The Lord our God is one Lord; and you shall love the Lord your God with all your heart, and with all your soul, and with all your might" (Deut. 6:4-5). But these words are to be more than intellectual beliefs: "And these words which I command you this day shall be upon your heart; and *you shall teach them diligently to your children,* and shall talk of them when you sit in your house, and when you walk by the way, and when you lie down, and when you rise" (Deut. 6:6-

7; italics mine). Indeed, the solidarity of the Jewish family and the responsibility of the parents to the upbringing of the children is still a hallmark of the Jewish home.

The Christian church, of course, built on this tradition. It is hardly necessary to remind ourselves of Jesus' training and the story of his being brought to the Temple at twelve. The passage from Ephesians mentioned earlier and the life of Timothy dramatize that Christian nurture is a most valid way of encountering God from the earliest days of the church. A little later, one of the greatest preachers of all times addressed himself to the passage in Ephesians 6:4. Chrysostom, in one of his famous homilies preserved to this day, states the need for nurture and the danger of being a solitary Christian:

Our own individual virtue is not enough in order to salvation. If the man who omitted to put out the one talent gained nothing, and yet was punished even then, it is plain that one's own individual virtue is not enough in order to salvation, but there is need of that of another also. Let us therefore entertain great solicitude for our wives, and take great care of our children, and of our servants, and of ourselves. And in our government both of ourselves and of them, let us beseech God that he aid us in the work.[4]

80

Bushnell, then, although his point of view was not the dominant one in the nineteenth century, nevertheless had Christian tradition on his side when he called for a faith that was the result of natural growth. What he affirmed was as old as the gospel and as new as the latest theories of psychology. His statement of a child growing up in an atmosphere so Christian that he never knows himself as being otherwise is a memorable idea. But this statement rests on some Christian views which are basic to the whole church, if not the entire Christian enterprise. For one thing, as has been indicated, he was seeing religion as more than a solitary matter between a man and his God. Further, he recognized the nature of the family as a social group and demonstrated how the spirit and character of parents influence inevitably the life and character of the children. In short, life in the family is a means of grace—a channel for the Holy Spirit. God uses the family to fulfill his promises.

It is to such views as these that we all subscribe who are in families and are participating in the life of the churches. Certainly, whether we think theologically about it or not, we hope our family life has the qualities which enable our children to develop naturally into the program of the church and into life with God. We send them to

81

church school for the same reason. It is our desire that they be nurtured in learning and in faith so that the advent into church membership will be a natural step toward their becoming mature Christians.

II

Although the limitations of the nurture approach to faith may not be so varied or apparent as in other types of Christian experience, the dangers are no less real. This approach should not be construed to mean that a child should grow into adulthood by joining the church in adolescence and never make a decision on his own. This approach does not preclude a decision made by the individual for the faith he is to assume. Undoubtedly, one of the reasons so many laymen in the church are dissatisfied with their faith is the fact that they "grew up" in the church but never really made a decision to become Christian. It is one thing to say that a person should grow up in the faith and become Christian in a natural way. It is something else to say that one becomes a Christian naturally without making a decision for the faith one assumes. What Bushnell was suggesting was that the decision for a Christian way of life did

82

not necessarily need to be soul-wrenching and cataclysmic along the lines of a revivalistic conversion.
But a decision for Christ is necessary for one to
be a Christian. How many churchmen are unhappy
over the lack of enthusiasm they have for the
church because they do not see that they have
never accepted on the deepest levels the vows they
recited by rote when they joined the church?

Close to this is the temptation to accept the parents' faith without appropriating it for ourselves.
The danger of living off the faith of our fathers is
plain. Yet the churches are full of people who have
had no satisfactory experience of their own but are
there simply because of the faith of their parents.
While that kind of faith is commendable—even
necessary according to the experience under discussion—if we have not made it our own, it is less
than satisfying. This temptation to live off the
parents' faith is accepting the fruit without the
roots, and such faith eventually withers and dies.

Above all, there is obviously a lack of satisfac-
tion in not having an experience of our own. No
one else can have our Christian experience for us.
A story is told of a bishop who was ordaining a
rather colorless candidate for the ministry. The
bishop was heard to remark, ''I think this young
man overheard another man's call to the minis-

83

try." Certainly there is a danger in "overhearing" or trying to live on another's Christian experience—even that of saintly parents.

III

In spite of the difficulties, the Christian nurture approach is the "ideal" we strive for in the Christian family—both home and church. The family should provide an atmosphere so Christian that we can see our children develop into mature Christians as a result of a natural process, not forgetting the necessity for them to make their own decisions as adult believers. For in a real sense the home is the arena where the gospel becomes the most concrete. It is a microcosm of the Christian faith. If the Christian message doesn't work here, it just doesn't work. For here we find sin, love, forgiveness, repentance, grace—all the essentials of the Christian gospel which will prepare the child for a mature Christian faith.

Closely allied to this concept of the home is the nurture of the church. It is provided in two ways. As we saw earlier, Bushnell emphasized the fact that the family itself could be a means of grace through which God worked. The church is related to the family in many ways, but in Bushnell's opinion one of the dramatic ways to see the family as the custodian of faith was through the practice of infant baptism. Whatever may be the theological basis for the rite, Bushnell saw it clearly as a symbol of the nurture approach to the faith: "Thus it is that infant baptism becomes an appropriate rite. It sees the child in the parent, counts him presumptively a believer and a Christian, and, with the parent, baptizes him also." [5]

If the home is related to the church as it dramatizes the gospel in miniature and is sealed through the baptism of the child, the Christian experience of nurture is further exemplified in the whole concept of the church school. Whatever else we may expect from the educational program of the church, we certainly expect our children to learn about the Christian gospel, understand the nature of the church, and develop psychologically in a wholesome manner—all the while growing "in wisdom and in stature, and in favor with God and man." The Sunday school program is based on the assumption that the psychological development of the child will be correlated to the growth in understanding of the Christian faith. Thus, all over Christendom, young people after years of Christian training and specific church membership enter into the life of the church and take their

85

place as fellow workers with those whom they continually replace in the leadership of the church. We parents—and this includes most of us—who have our children baptized and who send them to church school are affirming our support of the idea of Christian nurture. We know they will have to make the basic decision for themselves someday, but we want the years of church school—and the home—to be the preparation for a normal, natural advent into the kingdom of God.

Finally, if we were expressing our hopes for the ideal society, they too would reflect this approach to God—not in a sectarian manner, or with the church taking over the secular order or even the name Christian, perhaps. But from the standpoint of modern psychological development and learning theory, coupled with the necessity of stable family life—all seen under the fatherhood of a loving God—then it makes real sense to talk of a child becoming a Christian through nurture. We could very well place in our homes—and our churches—Bushnell's words: "The child is to grow up a Christian, and never know himself as being otherwise."

8

ALMOST CHRISTIANS

Suppose we decide to have our house completely redecorated. We have always wanted to have a professional decorator do it, and Aunt Emily has left us a little nest egg to make it possible. So, in a flush of excitement we go to Luigi, the best decorator in the city, and contract for the job. He is, of course, willing to do it, but he makes one stipulation: He must have complete control and absolute authority before he will put his name on the finished product. Excited as we are, we agree eagerly and wait expectantly for the day when the work begins. Luigi comes and begins the tour of our comfortable old home, jotting down suggestions as he moves from room to room. Out must go the comfortable horsehair couch; even Aunt Emily's portrait must come out of the hall; the old, familiar two-oven stove must be replaced. We gulp occasionally but nod as we proceed from room to room, seeing our most cherished possessions replaced by the professional decorator. At last we come to the comfortable den with the overstuffed leather chair and footstool, the pipe rack close at hand, slippers under the chair, restful, dark-panelled walls, and the wonderful old reading lamp with the green shade. Luigi purses his lips and furrows his brow. "This will have to go, too." "Oh, no," we cry, "this is my favorite hangout. I can't give this up." Luigi, remembering his contract, folds his notes, places them in his briefcase, and walks out. We are left standing alone in our comfortable den. We are unable to let go completely; we can't commit ourselves totally; we want part of our domain to be ours alone.

How many Christians could testify that this story is a picture of their own religious experience? How many of us—in all honesty—must confess that our own faith is of this same quality? We are not totally committed; we are almost Christians.

I

In the Gospel of Mark (12:28-34), there is the familiar story of a man who could not, did not, or would not totally commit himself. The encounter is with Jesus himself. The unknown scribe who approached Jesus was different from most of his antagonists. This man evidently came to Jesus to learn something—not to show off his own learning or to trap Jesus. It proves among other things that some of the Jews admired and appreciated Jesus. The scribe called him Teacher, a term of respect, and was sincerely seeking an answer to his question, "Which commandment is the first of all?" Jesus, for his part, seeing that the scribe was sincere, commended him for his knowledge and told him that he was not far from the kingdom. What was lacking was not right knowledge, nor perhaps even right living, but total commitment.

What had Jesus said that showed the scribe that he was close to the kingdom but not in it? Actually, it was rather simple; and for the religious man of the day trying to abide by innumerable religious laws, it could have been a welcomed relief. Jesus was telescoping into two commandments all the necessary requirements for a man to be truly religious. He took the very familiar Shema—the

89

daily prayer of the Jews that said we must love
God with all our heart, soul, mind, and strength—
and coupled with this the injunction to love our
neighbors as ourselves. The scribe himself agreed
that this total love of God (which was not a frag-
mentation of heart, soul, and mind, but a total
response) was much more than any kind of burnt
sacrifice. Love God and love neighbor. How simple! Then and now. Yet the scribe found himself
without the commitment. Not far from the kingdom, yet not in it. Jesus commended him for his
knowledge of the commandment. "You are not
far from the kingly rule of God in your life." [1]
All that was left was total commitment.

There is another encounter in Acts 26:1-32 between the multifaceted man, Paul, and King
Agrippa. Here is a stark contrast between Paul—
the committed—and Agrippa—the almost committed. Paul stood before the king, bound in chains
and on trial for his life. The apostle related himself to the king, who as a Jew knew all the laws
and religious customs of his subjects. Paul himself had been an antagonist of the Christians in his
days as a Pharisee, but after the blinding light experience on the Damascus road he had become the
great protagonist of the Christian faith. His commitment had become total, and when he talked

about his single-minded devotion, Festus interrupted the proceedings by saying categorically, "Paul, you are mad" (vs. 24*b*).

But Agrippa did not say that! He understood what Paul was saying. After all, Paul had addressed him directly and said, "King Agrippa, do you believe the prophets? I know that you believe" (vs. 27). Paul, in basing his Christian experience on the fulfillment of the prophetic utterances of the Old Testament, was trying to elicit the kind of understanding which sometimes results in a committed life. Agrippa retorted (in the King James Version), "Almost thou persuadest me to be a Christian" (vs. 28). The newer versions seem to give a different interpretation of this verse in their translations. The Revised Standard Version states, "In a short time you think to make me a Christian!" And the New English Bible has it, "You think it will not take much to win me over and make a Christian of me." These newer translations suggest that there is scorn and ridicule in the voice of Agrippa as he speaks to Paul. But, whatever the difficulties, it is clear to both Paul and the author, Luke, that Agrippa was undoubtedly moved by Paul's appeal. Agrippa did know a lot about religion. He might even have been a religious man, but in the midst of a momentous peri-

91

od in history he was a spectator. He may have been almost persuaded—almost Christian—but the small man who stood before him in chains was definitely persuaded. His commitment was total.

II

It is painful to point out the limitations of this approach to God, for in some ways it is the most autobiographical of all experiences of religion. We try to fool ourselves, however, by mixing up the cast of characters when we read the scripture passages. For example, we tend to align ourselves with Jesus or Paul rather than with the scribe or Agrippa. We are, too often, almost Christian.

Observers of the church in America make the charge of "almost Christian" about our Christianity as a whole. We have new buildings, relatively full churches, large budgets; we are near—yet so far. There are all the appearances of Christianity; yet much of our American faith is a superficial facade. The church is all too often a nondescript, vague form of the American way of life. It sometimes has chameleon-like tendencies, blending with the mores of the surrounding culture. In some cases the cross has been replaced by the weathervane to signify that the messages preached are dictated by the way in which the political and social winds are blowing. At times we have become an amiable religious service club which demands only a partial commitment.

The way the church loses its commitment and thus its mission can be illustrated in an analogy of a lifesaving station on the coast of Maine. It was built for rescue purposes. When a ship would wreck on the shoals of the North Atlantic, a few hardy souls would get into their old boat and row out to pick up survivors. They were committed to this task, and in time their fame spread. They decided that they should have a new boathouse. Some of the members decided that they would become honorary lifesavers and hired others to go out for rescue work. There was an auxiliary lifesaving chapter which served coffee and doughnuts, and whose members made flower beds in the shape of boats but never went to sea. They became so concerned about the trappings of lifesaving that they spent little or no time in the actual work of saving lives. They had lost their commitment.[2]

If such can become the state of the church as a whole, it is only because we Christians who make it up have lost our own commitment. We take neither the high road nor the low, but wander on the misty flats to and fro—failing to commit our-

93

selves completely. As J. S. Whale suggests, in the midst of burning bush experiences, instead of taking off our shoes, we take photographs from every suitable angle.[3] We are too content to be spectators —not committed. Could we imagine a surgeon pulling off his gloves at the end of a busy day and saying, "Well, three out of five. That's not a bad average"? We hope he is committed completely to 100 percent effort, especially if we happen to be fourth or fifth for the day.

Usually, though, we can handle our lack of commitment nicely. We simply think of someone else— not ourselves. But let us go back to the home decorator and the one room that cannot be given up. Isn't it true that most of us have a den or lair in the domiciles of our lives which keeps us from going all the way? It may be an uncontrollable temper; some secret vice; a concealed affair; a racial or religious prejudice; some feeling of guilt; a person we cannot forgive; some hate or malice; a nasty habit. We would like to be totally committed; yet we cannot give it up. It is too much a part of us. Even though we feel guilty about it, we are much too comfortable with it to give it up. And so we go along like a man in a tuxedo with

94

moccasins on his feet. We are not far from the kingdom; we are there—almost.

III

If there is a value in this type of experience, it comes when we try to move ourselves to more committed lives. But how do we move from *almost* Christian to *committed* Christian? In the first instance, facing up to ourselves is one way to get started. Knowledge of what we are is always a good way to get us going toward something else. But more than that, we need to remember that we cannot straighten up our own lives. We find it difficult to come to terms with our own tempers, or prejudices, or mean spirits. We cannot redecorate our houses professionally. However, our trust in God and commitment to him and his will can change our lives. When we give ourselves to him in faith and love and act accordingly toward our neighbors, then he can move us from the "almost" category to the "kingdom" category.

We are told that we cannot become good swimmers until we give ourselves to the water and have faith that it will buoy us up. One cannot be a good swimmer and go across the pool dragging one foot on the bottom. So it is with our Christian faith. It only means something when it costs something. That total Christian commitment which also brings total joy comes only when we give ourselves in complete trust to God who knows us and therefore can release us from our bondage to ourselves. When this has been done, then we are free to love not only him but our neighbors as well.

It is the same kind of commitment we undertake in marriage. One reason so many marriages have bogged down into a kind of tired friendship is that total commitment is lacking. A successful marriage is one where the partners have committed themselves totally to the relationship—holding back nothing (no secret rooms)—and live on the affirmation "from this day forward, . . . till death us do part." If that kind of faith can join us together as humans, how much more is it true that all-the-way faith in our relationship with God can lead to wholly committed lives?

The results of a totally committed life are easy to see. This is no perfectionism or insipid idealism. It simply means that we are to remember that we are the church. No one else is. We are God's men and women called to do his work. If we really believe that, it might scare us; but it would change our lives. It means that God is point North on our compass. He transcends our other loyalties, whatever they are. We ask the question, in every situation, "What would God have me to do?" Not my political party or my natural predisposition, or my club or my business or even my family—but what would God have *me* do? A good test for a Christian might be this: "How has being a Christian changed my mind? My life? What thing that I prefer to do or think as my 'natural' inclination has had to be changed because of being a Christian?" It is this kind of commitment that takes the "almost" away from the designation "Christian."

Someone has reminded us that in high school geometry each of us used to have a compass with a point on one leg and a pencil holder on the other. At the fulcrum there was a degree scale, and we could draw circles by setting the scale, placing the point on the paper, and swinging the pencil leg in a clockwise motion. There was one catch—the center had to be set down steadily and held firmly for the circle to be exactly true. How true that is in our lives: if the center is right, the circumference will take care of itself. If we are totally committed to love of God and neighbor, then the rest will be placed in a proper perspective.

The Archbishop of Canterbury once commented that the world was made up of three groups of

97

people: Communists, convinced Christians, and amiable nonentities. Our task in life—in terms of our Christian experience—is to move through God's grace from the category of "amiable nonentity" to the one labeled "convinced Christian."

9

OUTSIDER CHRISTIANS

In our day we hear a great deal about the Christian who is outside the church. Presumably, this means that there are those who are committed to the Christian faith but who have no formal relationship with the institutional church. Further, it might also include those who are outside the church and have no particular commitment at all to the religious life, but whose actions make them brothers to the man of faith. We even see such terms as "secular Christian" and "religionless Christianity" used as attempts to describe the life of concerned people outside the institutional church.

It is not easy to use one term to describe the

outsider. For one thing, there are theological considerations at stake in contrasting the visible with the invisible church. For another, the word "outsider" refers more to a state of being rather than to geography. For this reason, it is helpful to see some definition of what is meant by "outsider." James E. Sellers has attempted to clarify our thinking in a most penetrating way. He describes the ambiguity of the word when he says:

It is not an ideal term, for in a sense we are *all* outsiders to the Word of God. Yet it does have the merit of suggesting the most difficult thing about Christian communication, which is the fact that so many people stand, in effect, beyond or outside the church, preoccupied with other voices, other values.[1]

The outsider, then, is not only outside the church; sometimes he may even sit in the pews. Also, he may not only be "preoccupied with other . . . values," he may even be preoccupied with the same values but still choose to remain outside the fellowship of believers.

I

Such a diverse concept of religious experience obviously would reflect various examples. Fortunately, the Bible is replete with prototypes of the outsider Christian, dramatizing among other things the contemporaneous nature of the biblical witness. But also the variety.

For example, one of the most fascinating accounts in the Bible occurs in the Gospel of Matthew when Jesus meets the woman who has a daughter possessed by a demon (15:21-28; cf. Mark 5:25-34). She was a Canaanite woman—a definite outsider—who yet recognized in Jesus the power to bring healing to her daughter. She was a foreigner, and Jesus' reply to her is puzzling, for he states that his primary mission is to the lost sheep of Israel—not gentiles. He even gives her a saying which on the surface seems cruel and unwarranted. He states that it is not fair to take the children's bread and throw it to the dogs. Some believe this is a popular saying Jesus adopted for the occasion, meaning, of course, that the "children" were the Jews and the "dogs" were the gentiles. This rebuff is not as bad as it sounds if, as some think, Jesus—at least at this time—conceived of his mission as being only to the Jewish people themselves. At any rate, the woman answered with another quip that even the dogs eat the crumbs that fall from their master's table. Jesus was impressed with this outsider's faith,

101

WHICH WAY TO GOD?

and it is reported he healed her daughter instantly. The foreigner had faith in Jesus' ability to help, even though she herself was an outsider.

Such experiences can be duplicated many times in the New Testament. Take, for example, the centurion at the Crucifixion. Here was definitely an outsider—one who led the soldiers who crucified Jesus. When he and his men who witnessed the death of Jesus "saw the earthquake and what took place, they were filled with awe, and said, 'Truly this was a son of God!' " (Matt. 27:54). The passage in Mark is similar, but in Luke he even declared that "this man was innocent!" (Luke 23:47). Charles Rann Kennedy, in his play *The Terrible Meek,* dramatizes for us the impact that Jesus had on this Roman soldier. At one point the captain exclaims, "He's alive. I can't kill him. All the empires can't kill him." [2] The incident lends itself to such dramatization, for the soldier with his pagan faith saw a man die gloriously like a Roman demigod. He was so much impressed that even from the outside he made what the disciples must have felt was a confession of faith. Jesus had become a triumphant and even a divine hero to the very one who put him to death.

Or take the story of Peter and Cornelius in Acts 10. Here is another soldier who, although an outsider, was not a pagan. He was devout, gave alms, and even prayed. He became the instrument by which Peter saw the necessity of relating the gospel to the gentiles as well as the Jews. After Peter's vision of a broadened concept of God's plan of salvation, Cornelius convinced Peter that God had made him a part of his plan to reveal the breadth of the gospel. Peter was convinced and preached a sermon to the assembled on the universality of Christ's person and work. At the end of the sermon Cornelius and the others were baptized and became a part of the Christian community. In a real sense, here is a most dramatic account of an outsider who became an insider.

Another graphic account of an encounter with an outsider concerns Peter again in Acts 5. Here the outsider is Gamaliel, a Pharisee. What type was more removed from the Christians than the Pharisees? Yet when Peter and the other apostles were dragged before the council, Gamaliel, a teacher of the law and a member of the council, protected them. Indeed, he told the council to let the Christians alone and offered some timeless advice: "Keep away from these men and let them alone; for if this plan or this undertaking is of men, it will fail; but if it is of God, you will not be able to overthrow them. You might even be found opposing God!'' (vss. 38-39). We read that the council took Gamaliel's advice, and even though they received a beating, the disciples left the council rejoicing and went on teaching and preaching. Gamaliel was an outsider to the Christian faith, but he was not about to thwart God's will. If the preaching of the gospel were nonsense, it would fall of its own accord. If it had God's backing, it would be dangerous to stand in its way. This outsider saw with sympathetic eyes what was unfolding before him.

An extreme form of the outsider occurs in the Gospels in the relationship between Jesus and the people possessed by demons. These incidents raise a lot of related questions concerning demonology, healing, miracles, and so forth. One fascinating conjecture is that it seems for Mark, at least, that there was something occult in the fact that the demons recognized Jesus as holy even when others, including the disciples, did not. This may be Mark's way of explaining the obtuseness of the disciples in not being more faithful.

In the first chapter of Mark there is a story of a man with an unclean spirit who accosted Jesus and recognized him, calling him the Holy One of God. Jesus healed him, and the people were amazed that he could evict the evil spirits. It is significant for our purpose that Mark believed the man recognized the divinity of Jesus. This is the insight of the nonrespectable—the outsider. Although the title "Holy One of God" may not have meant the same to the man as it did to Mark, it nevertheless served as a vehicle for Mark's contention that the demons had the power to recognize the supernatural qualities of Jesus.

An equally arresting incident occurs in Mark 5, when Jesus enters the territory of the Gerasenes. Here he is met by a madman strong enough to break chains, who lives in tombs and is filled with so many spirits that he refers to himself as Legion, or many. Here again, the man recognizes Jesus for what he is, calling him the Son of the Most High God. Jesus commands the spirits to come out, which they do by entering a herd of swine and hurtling them into the sea. The demoniac was cured and began to proclaim abroad what Jesus had done for him.

What these biblical incidents—plus many others which could be cited—demonstrate is that there is a variety of people apart from the fellowship of the church who can be called outsiders. At first, we are tempted to think only of the hordes of people in the world who have nothing to do with the church or what she stands for. In a sense, of

105

course, these are the true outsiders, and this has a great deal to say about the church's role in evangelism. For all purposes here, however, we need to remind ourselves of the outsiders not normally thought religious who nevertheless act upon religious principles. These may be those who are thoroughly secular as far as separation from the visible body of believers is concerned. Or they may be outsiders who wistfully wish they could be on the inside but through conviction (or perhaps because of the hypocrisy they see in Christian churchmen) cannot be members of the church. Occasionally, even, these outsiders may sit in the pews of our churches but never really feel a part of the embracing fellowship.

II

It is easy for most of us to see the difficulties inherent in a religious experience which is outside the fellowship. That inadequacy—in others—we are quick to point out. Yet there is enough of the outsider in us all that we need to remind ourselves of the inadequacy of trying to maintain our Christian experience from the vantage point of a non-participant.

106

The first temptation of the one who desires to remain on the outside may be rationalization for not identifying with the church. Although Simone Weil was undoubtedly sincere when she wrote to a friend about her noninvolvement, many of us would not be when we say with her:

It seems to me that the will of God is that I should not enter the church at present. I cannot help still wondering whether in these days when so large a proportion of humanity is submerged in materialism, God does not want there to be some men and women who have given themselves to him and to Christ and who yet remain outside the church.[3]

Her point is well taken, but how many of us are on the outside for such serious reasons?

The tragedy of the Christian experience which is outside is that the Christian faith needs the fellowship with others who are committed. It is no accident that the church is the *body* of Christ, the *people* of God. No one worships God alone—easily. A person may say that he or she worships God in the rose garden or on the golf course or in the fishing boat, but we must be wary of such expressions. Although we do not know where God is (and he certainly cannot be confined in the four walls of an

107

ecclesiastical building), we should expect to find him where other Christians are gathered in his name to hear his Word read and proclaimed; where his praises are sung; and where his people pray together. Further, we need to test the reality of our experience of God. This is no rigid orthodoxy; it simply means that any subjective feeling of religion needs to be shared in the group of Christians to test its reality. Many of my "outside expressions" of faith may not be real experiences of faith after all. Worshiping in the body of believers helps us to see the true nature of Christian experience.

In short, the outsider needs the fellowship of other committed Christians; for he depends upon the nourishment of that body for his experience of faith, and he needs other believers for the continuing growth of his experience.

III

As with the other experiences of God, we can learn a great deal from the outsider's experience. For one thing, it reminds us that we cannot limit the ways or places in which God reveals himself. Arnold Toynbee reminds us of the pervasiveness of the Christian gospel into the very fabric of our society:

When Descartes and Voltaire and Marx and Machiavelli and Hobbes and Mussolini and Hitler have done their best to dechristianize our Western life, we may still suspect that their scouring and fumigating has been only partially effective. The Christian virus or elixir is in our Western blood.[4]

If we take Toynbee seriously, then it seems there is no outside for most of us, since the Christian message is in the structures of our lives.

But aside from this general conception of the outsider's experience we need to admit that often the outsider is closer to God than the insider. For example, many people have pointed to the fact that professional sports did more than the church to further the cause of civil rights in race relations. Few remember that Branch Rickey, who broke baseball's color line, was a devout churchman as well as a sports executive. The outsider does bring judgment on our own faith when he acts in a Christian way without the commitment we church-men are supposed to have. The relationship of this insight to the prodigal son story is painfully clear. The elder brother is judged harshly while the

109

younger son (the outsider) is received safe and sound.

Some of us may even need to redefine our understanding of the church, or the way God works among men. Our God may be too small, or our view of the church may be too narrow or exclusive. Today we hear a lot about secular Christianity. Without endeavoring to embrace that vague concept, one can point out that God still works in mysterious ways his wonders to perform—even in the crassly secular. Karl Barth reminds us that "God may speak to us through a pagan or an atheist, and in that way give us to understand that the boundary between church and the profane still and repeatedly takes a course quite different from that which we hitherto thought we saw." [5]

In any event, we must learn that we cannot capture or limit him. Our definition of the "inside" may be too constrictive. For, unbelievable as it may seem, *Jesus himself was an outsider*. Think of his relationship with his own family; with the religious leaders of the day; with the paganism of the Roman Empire. See through history how the spirit of Christ has been outside trying to get into places of power, men's minds, politicians' actions, men's hearts. Look at the cross and see what being an outsider cost. When we see that even our Master was outside the established orders of religion, then we can be more sympathetic to those who are not within the fellowship. Our task then becomes to live the kind of witness that will persuade the outsider to change the address of his spiritual residence.

10

ANONYMOUS CHRISTIANS

The contemporary Roman Catholic theologian Karl Rahner is responsible for bringing into our religious vocabularies the term "anonymous Christian." In a book based upon Rahner's concept, Anita Röper defines anonymous Christianity:

For by anonymous Christianity we mean that Christianity which is unaware of itself, which does not understand itself *as* Christianity. . . . We must expect to find Christian elements outside explicit Christianity, whether as the anonymous Christianity of the individual or as the strange phenomenon of a collective anonymous Christianity of whole nations.[1]

It is apparent that in many ways there are similarities between the anonymous Christian and the

112

outsider Christian. Yet there are distinctions, as will be seen. At this point, it is enough to note that the hallmark of the anonymous Christian is his unawareness of his stance. He is a person (or a group, perhaps) who is acting Christianly whether he knows it or not.

I

The most arresting biblical example of the anonymous Christian is the Last Judgment passage in Matthew 25:31-46. Here is the story of the judgment which places the sheep on the right hand and the goats on the left. Those on the right will inherit the kingdom because they fed the Son of man when he was hungry, gave him a drink when he was thirsty, welcomed him when he was a stranger, clothed him when he was naked, visited him when he was sick and in prison. The righteous are astounded. They don't remember seeing him hungry or thirsty, as a stranger, naked or in prison. But the King insists, "Truly, I say to you, as you did it to one of the least of these my brethren, you did it to me" (vs. 40). Conversely, those on the left did not minister to him when he was hungry, thirsty, naked, sick, in prison, and a stranger. They too are astounded, for they don't remember seeing their Lord in these conditions. Here again, though, they failed to minister to one of "the least of these" and thereby failed to minister to him.

It appears from this story that what one affirms or the label he wears—however pious—will be to no avail if he does not minister to his brother in need. On the other hand, the one who ministers to one in need, regardless of his affiliations or beliefs, will be serving the Lord as well—whether he knows it or not. Sherman C. Johnson has written of this incident:

The most striking note of the parable is that on Judgment Day some men will discover that, although they have not known it, they have been on God's side all the time. One of the characteristics of the true saint is that he forgets himself in service of God and man.[2]

This interpretation of the parable points up what could be the special quality of the anonymous Christian—on God's side, but not knowing it.

Although the passage in Matthew illustrates most clearly the attributes of the unknown or unknowing Christian, there are other people and incidents which fall under the same heading. One of the most touching is the role of Joseph of Arimathea after the Crucifixion of Jesus (John 19:38-

42). This Joseph was an influential Jew, a Pharisee and a member of the Sanhedrin. He asked for the body of Jesus, and tradition has it that he buried Jesus in his own family tomb. Scholars have speculated about the various motives that would persuade a leading Jew to pay this respect to Jesus and thus run the risk of condemnation from his countrymen. One of the most persistent traditions is that Joseph of Arimathea was a "secret" disciple of Jesus who came out into the open. If so, this is a case of an anonymous Christian who decided to make his faith known.

The centurion whose slave Jesus healed was another who might be considered an anonymous believer (Luke 7:1-10). He was a worthy man who had built a synagogue for the Jews. When Jesus came, the man protested that he was not worthy to have Jesus under his roof; yet he had the faith that Jesus could say the word and heal his slave. Jesus was impressed with the man's faith and healed the servant. Was this an anonymous Christian?

There are others who could be cited as possible examples of this category: the woman who touched the fringe of Jesus' garment, feeling that this act alone would bring her healing. Or the man who sought healing for his child, perhaps not having

115

enough belief, but crying "I believe; help my unbelief!" This could well be the stance of an anonymous Christian who believes and doubts.

Whatever the variations, they are variations on the same theme. The concept of the anonymous Christian causes us to reevaluate our rigid views of who is or is not religious. We can understand the dimension of the anonymous Christian when we view what was at one time an arrogant missionary posture of taking Christ to Africa or China. One writer makes clear another way of regarding other peoples: "Christ was already in China or Africa long before a single missionary set foot there. Christ was part of the structure of other faiths, of other cultures, of art, of family and social life, of the individual's thinking and feeling." [3] Such a view—unusual as it may seem to some—illustrates admirably both the nature of the one who is an anonymous Christian and the scope of God's work in Christ.

Father Donceel, a Jesuit priest, makes an even more trenchant case for the anonymous Christian. He states that the Christian enterprise is pitifully small only if we overlook those millions of anonymous Christians who live among us as they live among Hindus, Moslems, and behind the Iron Curtain. These are people who may never have heard

116

of Jesus Christ or, if they have, often reflect a fuzzy or distorted picture of him; yet they have welcomed him into the hidden depths of their hearts. ''These are the countless millions of humble people who, all over the earth, live according to their lights, these are the 'men of good will.' '' [4] Christians have often called ''men of good will'' allies in the cause of justice and righteousness, but Father Donceel considers them Christian in their own right.

II

The weakness of the anonymous Christian's experience is not as easily identifiable as in other types discussed. The very anonymity makes the person unaware that he either is living or should be living a specific Christian way of life. His is a nameless religion in many cases; most often he is an unconscious Christian at best.

To see this idea clearly, we must stretch our minds to see a completely different framework of God's work with man. Emil Brunner helps us to see something of the magnitude of this category when he speaks of the orders of creation. To Brunner, what we often call the laws of nature are really God's orders of creation. A man who does

117

not profess to know God may have a vast knowledge of his orders of creation without knowing him. For example, the scientist or mathematician may subscribe to laws of nature which are really God's laws. "Thus, without knowing anything of the true Creator, man may know the orders and laws of the Creator without knowing whose laws they are." [5]

Thus, while as Christians we might want to say that everyone should confess the Lord Jesus Christ as his Savior, yet the fact is that millions do not; and we should be grateful to have our horizons broadened to see that no one is beyond God's love and care—whatever label he may carry. Karl Rahner himself reminds us that the man of the "extra-Christian" religion is not merely a non-Christian; he is already an anonymous Christian. And this would be true even for the man of no faith. "It would be false to consider the pagan a man untouched by God's grace and truth." [6]

Although the Christian can be grateful for the experience of the anonymous Christian and for the knowledge that God's creative work is universal, yet with the revelation he has he is enjoined to confess the name of Christ and to labor for his kingdom. For we who have been given specific knowledge of God's will have no other alternative

118

but to witness to God's love in Christ in our own lives and to our neighbors.

To those not of the fellowship of believers—including, of course, the anonymous Christians—our task is to make known to them the unknown God they worship and to live worthy lives so they too will want to be part of the Christian fellowship. The unity of the body of Christ is our goal, and we should be concerned that all men of faith make their undivided, collective testimony to the one God. To this end, we continue to witness that all may be one by making their beliefs active and by becoming visible followers of the God who is the Creator and Sustainer of all mankind.

III

Still, we can be grateful for the spirit of our ecumenical age which enables us to understand other aspects of faith than our own and to lessen our narrow views of what the church is or where God is. Apart from the new spirit of openness toward others, the cognizance of the anonymity of God's revelation places a different emphasis upon much of our Christian outreach. For example, the evangelistic message may be seen in a new

119

light. Karl Rahner again gives the clue to such evangelism:

In the last analysis the preaching of the gospel does not make a Christian of a man completely abandoned by God and Christ, but transforms an anonymous Christian into a man who within the grace-filled depths of his nature is conscious of his Christianity objectively and reflectively as well as in a socially constituted profession thereof, in the Church.[7]

The purpose of preaching here, then, is to make him aware of the faith that is within him and to turn him into one conscious of his place in Christ's church.

This particular kind of experience shows us the all-inclusive work of God, which should be a comfort to Christians—knowing that they worship a God who is not too small. Further, such an experience should be judgment on our sometimes too narrow understanding of what the church is and who is a Christian. We often penalize our witness by our dogmatism and intemperate spirits. Why is it that so often the one outside the church is so much more attractive than the Christian himself? Bonhoeffer sensed this for many of us when he wrote: "I often ask myself why a Christian instinct frequently draws me more to the religionless than to the religious, by which I mean not any intention of evangelizing them, but rather, I might almost say, in 'brotherhood.' '' [8] This drawing to the religionless in brotherhood is a mandate for the Christian in terms his own spirit of love, and because of the knowledge that this one is within God's circle of care—at least, anonymously.

It is also exciting for the Christian to remember that the same God who is the Father of our Lord Jesus Christ is at work in the faith of the Jews, the Buddhists, and other men who worship in their different ways—exciting because it reminds us again that the God we worship created and sustains the whole universe. We do not worship a sectarian, parochial, or national God who is the extension of our own desires. The God we worship is not made by human hands and therefore cannot be manipulated by human hands. He is *in* all and *through* all, doing his work in a multitude of ways and in a variety of places. This does not mean our witness is changed. Indeed, we are called upon as Christians to live up to the faith we know. It does mean, however, that our experience is acted out against a backdrop of God's manifold expressions in history. Schubert Ogden sees the Christian's task clearly in this regard:

To be sure, the church stands by the claim that the decisive manifestation of this divine word is none other than the human word of Jesus of Nazareth and thence of its own authentic proclamation. But the point of this claim is not that the Christ is manifest only in Jesus and nowhere else, but that the word addressed to men *everywhere,* in all the events of their lives, is none other than the word spoken in Jesus and in the preaching and sacraments of one church.[9]

The Christian stands by his claim of the richness of his Christian experience. He further affirms that the anonymous spirit in the lives of men everywhere is the same God who is the Father of his Lord Jesus Christ and whose will for all men is that they might be one.

NOTES

1. Pioneer Christians

1. Cf. the article "John the Baptist" in *The Interpreter's Dictionary of the Bible* (Nashville: Abingdon Press, 1962), p. 955.

2. Prodigal Christians

1. See *The Interpreter's Bible* (Nashville: Abingdon Press, 1953-1957), VII, 568-70.
2. *Ibid.*, p. 868. Read the entire exposition of Mark 14:3-9 (pp. 868-71).
3. *The Interpreter's Bible*, VIII, 141.
4. *Ibid.*, pp. 142-43.
5. *The Interpreter's Bible*, VII, 853.
6. Quoted in *The Interpreter's Bible*, VIII, 360.
7. T. S. Eliot, *The Cocktail Party*, in *Complete Poems and Plays*, p. 363. Reprinted by permission of Harcourt, Brace & World and Faber & Faber.
8. *The Interpreter's Bible*, VII, 868.

4. EMOTIONAL CHRISTIANS

1. Williston Walker, *A History of the Christian Church* (New York: Charles Scribner's Sons, 1947), p. 177.

5. SHALLOW CHRISTIANS

1. The details of Judas' death vary. We are here using the account in Matt. 26:20-25, 47-50; 27:3-5. The Gospels tell us that Judas committed suicide. The details of his death do not matter.
2. See the excellent article "Judas" in *The Interpreter's Dictionary of the Bible*, p. 1006.
3. Tom Paine, *The American Crisis.*
4. Nikos Kazantzakis, *The Greek Passion* (New York: Ballantine Books, 1955), p. 32.
5. *Ibid.*

6. INTELLECTUAL CHRISTIANS

1. *Phillips Brooks on Preaching* (New York: The Seabury Press, 1964), p. 44.
2. *Ibid.,* p. 45.
3. *The Interpreter's Bible*, IX, 114.
4. *Ibid.,* p. 232.
5. Horace Bushnell, *Christian Nurture*, ed. Luther A. Weigle (New Haven: Yale University Press, 1953), pp. 11-12.
6. *The Interpreter's Bible*, IX, 232.
7. *Ibid.*

7. NURTURED CHRISTIANS

1. *Christian Nurture*, p. 4.
2. *The Interpreter's Bible*, XI, 463. Dr. Gealy seems to indicate that the face value supposition can be taken, since "Acts 16:1 [where Timothy and his lineage are mentioned] does not exclude this possibility."
3. *Ibid.*

4. Chrysostom, Homily xxi, *A Library of Fathers of the Holy Catholic Church*, VI, 345.
5. *Christian Nurture*, p. 30.

8. ALMOST CHRISTIANS

1. Another way of stating the nature of the kingdom of God.
2. Theodore Wedel, "Evangelism—The Mission of the Church to Those Outside Her Life," *The Ecumenical Review*, October, 1953, p. 24.
3. J. S. Whale, *Christian Doctrine* (London: Fontana Books, 1957), p. 146.

9. OUTSIDER CHRISTIANS

1. James E. Sellers, *The Outsider and the Word of God* (Nashville: Abingdon Press, 1961), p. 8.
2. Charles Rann Kennedy, *The Terrible Meek* (New York: Harper & Brothers, 1912), p. 37.
3. *Waiting for God*, trans. Emma Craufurd (New York: G. P. Putnam's Sons, 1951), pp. 47-48. Quoted in John Killinger, *The Failure of Theology in Modern Literature* (Nashville: Abingdon Press, 1963), p. 84.
4. *A Study of History*, Vols. I-VI abridged by D. C. Somervell (New York: Oxford University Press, 1947), I, 400-401. Quoted in Sellers, *The Outsider and the Word of God*, p. 16.
5. *Church Dogmatics I/1*, trans. G. T. Thomson (Edinburgh: T. & T. Clark, 1960), pp. 60-61. Quoted in Killinger, *The Failure of Theology in Modern Literature*, p. 13.

10. ANONYMOUS CHRISTIANS

1. Anita Roper, *The Anonymous Christian*, tr. Joseph Donceel (New York: Sheed and Ward, 1966), p. 12.
2. *The Interpreter's Bible*, VII, 562.
3. Monica Furlong in *The Restless Church*, ed. William Kilbourn (Philadelphia: J. B. Lippincott Co., 1966), p. 43.

4. J. Donceel, Preface in Roper, *The Anonymous Christian*, p. *v*.
5. Emil Brunner, *The Christian Doctrine of Creation and Re-demption* [*Dogmatics*, Vol. II], trans. Olive Wyon (Philadelphia: The Westminster Press, 1952), p. 26.
6. Karl Rahner, "Christianity and Non-Christian Religions," in *The Church*, ed. Hugo Rahner (New York: P. J. Kenedy & Sons, 1963), p. 131.
7. *Ibid.*, p. 132.
8. Dietrich Bonhoeffer, *Letters and Papers from Prison*, ed. Eberhard Bethge and trans. R. H. Fuller (New York: The Macmillan Company, 1953), p. 165.
9. Schubert Ogden, *Christ Without Myth* (New York: Harper & Row, 1961), p. 156.

WHICH
WAY
TO
GOD?

Ronald E. Sleeth

People are not alike, and their ways
to God are not alike.

This book for laymen takes a close
look at some of the many approaches
to God. It demonstrates the variety of
approaches seen in the Bible, indicat-
ing their strengths and weaknesses. As
he looks at their present-day counter-
parts, Dr. Sleeth vividly shows the im-
mense richness of Christian experience.

Which Way to God? will encourage
a broadening and deepening of the
reader's own religious experience and
should lead to the understanding that
mature religion may encompass many
different aspects of faith. ''The main
thing is that God works in many ways.
He takes us where we are. He calls us
to grow in our own experience.''

As the author looks at each type of
approach—the intellectual, the emo-